BRINGING *the* RAINBOW

BRINGING *the* RAINBOW

—The Hindware Story—

R.K. SOMANY

MAVEN
RUPA

Published in Maven by
Rupa Publications India Pvt. Ltd 2016
7/16, Ansari Road, Daryaganj
New Delhi 110002

Sales Centres:
Allahabad Bengaluru Chennai
Hyderabad Jaipur Kathmandu
Kolkata Mumbai

Copyright © R.K. Somany 2016

The events are portrayed to the best of the author's recall and understanding.
The conversations are not written verbatim.
The views and opinions expressed in this book are the author's own and the facts are as reported by him which have been verified to the extent possible, and the publishers are not in any way liable for the same.

All rights reserved.
No part of this publication may be reproduced, transmitted, or stored in a retrieval system, in any form or by any means, electronic, mechanical, photocopying, recording or otherwise, without the prior permission of the publisher.

ISBN: 978-81-291-4211-5

First impression 2016

10 9 8 7 6 5 4 3 2 1

The moral right of the author has been asserted.

This book is sold subject to the condition that it shall not, by way of trade or otherwise, be lent, resold, hired out, or otherwise circulated, without the publisher's prior consent, in any form of binding or cover other than that in which it is published.

To my mother Janki Devi Somany

CONTENTS

Prologue ix

1. My earliest recollections 1
2. Education and my formative years 8
3. My eldest brother, my *loco parentis* 23
4. Initiation into business 34
5. My hobbies and interests 51
6. Taking a risk: A new beginning 60
7. My personal life 77
8. Giving back to society 99
9. From newbie to market leader 117
10. Family feud and partition 137
11. Economic liberalization of 1991: New challenges, new opportunities 156
12. My work ethic and business philosophy 166
13. My idols 177
14. The way forward 190

Acknowledgements 201

PROLOGUE

It was 30 December 1959, the eve of the new decade. Soon there would be the excitement of celebrations in Delhi, but at the time, my wife and I were lulled into half-sleep by the clacking of the train. We were on our way from Calcutta (Kolkata) for a cousin's wedding.

It is said that life is full of surprises—and I was to discover that soon after reaching Delhi. Landing amidst the festivities, the wedding celebrations compounded by the revelries for the new year, I would be starting what would become one of the greatest adventures of my life.

Ashoka Hotel, where we were staying, laid out a rich spread, even organizing a separate kitchen for the many wedding guests who, like us, were strict vegetarians. My wife was "captured" by the other women of the family and I was considering my social options when Bhaiji—my eldest brother, now touching the ripe age of 96—called from Calcutta. Long-distance calls were a rarity in those days and my first reaction was anxiety.

Bhaiji quickly allayed my fears and moved on to the reason for the call. There were negotiations on for buying some land in Bahadurgarh in Punjab (now in Haryana). Some of the land had already been purchased but, suddenly and unexpectedly, farmers owning acreage in the middle of the area we sought were refusing to sell. Bhaiji said the farmers were probably holding out for an unreasonably large compensation and he wanted me to look into the matter and find a way out of the stalemate.

The next morning I set off for Bahadurgarh. I got myself an old Morris Minor and drove myself; we had no driver in Delhi; the car had no air-conditioning, no power-steering; it was old. Today, the 38-km drive along NH 10 (National Highway 10) is a breeze. At that time, it was along rutted mud roads, the bouncing old Morris Minor shaking my bones with every rotation of its wheels.

As I was fretting, I saw a rainbow appear on the horizon and the drive suddenly turned beautiful. A chore became exciting. That was my moment of epiphany. The rainbow became my guiding mantra. In whatever I do, as a businessperson, a father, a husband, a friend and a family man, I ask myself: 'Am I bringing the rainbow to this? The passion, the excitement, the colour?'

I reached Bahadurgarh to an obstinate standoff, a deadlock that did not let up after several attempts at negotiation over a tiresome three weeks, with just my always-present stock of Perry Mason murder mysteries to provide much-needed diversion. No offer sufficed and no demand stayed constant. The farmers could not understand what industrial development would mean, how it could benefit them. And someone was brewing trouble by spreading rumours about how we were acting for India's largest business house then, and had—what would now be termed—'deep pockets'.

BRINGING THE RAINBOW

Finally, I suggested to Bhaiji that we seek government help. By a fortuitous coincidence, the then chief minister of Punjab, Pratap Singh Kairon, was visiting a plant in Serampore in West Bengal and Bhaiji met him there. On learning of our troubles at Bahadurgarh, that great visionary leader, who laid the foundations for modern Punjab, Haryana and Himachal Pradesh, who famously told Jawaharlal Nehru, 'Don't meddle in my state', and who was then also the minister for industrial development for the united Punjab province, said, simply: *'Chalo ji, ho gaya!'* ['It's okay, sir, it's done!']

And, thus, the Bahadurgarh plant was conceived. The birthing process had its own pains, however. Though the government had ordered that the land would be acquired for industrial development, the papers moved slowly, numerous trunk calls were made, and ultimately, we had to appoint one person to be at hand in the administrative offices to actually just carry the papers from table to table...within and between Chandigarh, Jhajjar and Rohtak! Finally, we were the proud owners of 95 acres allocated for our glassware and sanitaryware manufacturing plants.

It was a long way from home in Calcutta, and the time I spent there was a lesson in combating homesickness, too! The discipline instilled in me by the Christian priests at St Xavier's Collegiate School, Calcutta, helped, as it has throughout my life, in everything I do, as have the moral science lessons taught in my missionary school.

These lessons have come together to instil in me the sense of what 'corporate citizenship' means—to repay those who have given us so much, be it the investors, the employees, the local community that supports our operations or society at large, that fosters our well-being.

R.K. SOMANY

That was the beginning of the great adventure that has been my association with Hindware!

The events in this book are portrayed to the best of my recollection and understanding.

1

MY EARLIEST RECOLLECTIONS

The early years of the twentieth century were a time of great hope and greater adventure. Many an intrepid Marwari lad were leaving their arid homeland in Rajasthan for Calcutta and Bombay (as these great metropolises were then called) in search of fame and fortune. Many achieved their ambitions, going on to become, even then, household names in the world of business and commerce.

My grandfather, Ram Prasad, and his brother, Mahadev, were two such men. Though the Somanys were a well-to-do family in Chirawa, in the Jhunjhunu district of Rajasthan, Ram Prasad was consumed with the ambition of achieving something bigger. We had a thriving moneylending business, some agricultural fields, our own haveli, and the family was well respected throughout the Shekhawati region. However, there wasn't much scope for growth in Chirawa. My grandfather and his brother longed to find a place where they could fulfil their ambitions.

In 1905–6, grandfather and his brother moved to Calcutta. It was a brave decision. At that time, Kanpur, the nearest railhead, almost 600 km away, could be reached only on camelback. It was a long and arduous journey, which took weeks. From there, grandfather boarded a train to Calcutta, the city that was to become home for him and his descendants for more than a century. Even today, I maintain strong links with Kolkata: all my companies are still registered in that city, though I moved to Delhi in 1961.

I have no idea how grandfather and his brother started out in what was to them a new and strange city. I have no idea if they knew anyone in Calcutta or where they stayed when they first reached the city. There are no records of their activities and much of what I know is based on hearsay and family lore. What is known is that they started a trading firm by the name of Ram Prasad Mahadev, which dabbled in opium (which was legal in those days!), raw jute and hessian, and prospered. Soon, the brothers amassed a small fortune.

Within a few years, though, they decided to go their own separate ways. Again, no one in the family knows why they took this decision, but by all accounts, it was an amicable parting. The firm was then rechristened Ram Prasad Murlidhar & Co—Murlidhar being my father.

My grandfather was a public-spirited individual who wanted to share his good fortune with his community. So in 1915, he set up the Chirawa Senior Secondary School in his village to provide education to the youth of his native region. The school is in its centenary year and is still run by our family.

As the business grew, the family diversified into stock trading.

My father, Murlidhar Somany, who had been adopted by my grandfather after his own son died, and my eldest brother Hiralall, started a brokerage firm by the name of Murlidhar Hiralall, which was to remain one of the main pillars of the family's fortune till we exited the business in the 1950s.

The Somanys were, by this time, counted among the well-respected and reputed Marwari families in Calcutta. The family had moved into its own house at 34B Ratu Sirkar Lane off Chittaranjan Avenue. It was quite a grand house by the standards of that time—a four-storey structure, with ten rooms on each floor, marble flooring, and high ceilings adorned with majestic chandeliers The ground floor housed the *gaddi* (office) and the garages, while the higher floors were our living quarters. Readers today may find it quaint, but in keeping with the practice of those days, there were no attached baths. For ablutions and other matters of personal hygiene, one had to walk to a set of toilets and baths at one end of each floor.

It was in this house that I was born, on 10 November 1937, the ninth among eleven children—eight brothers and three sisters. In those days, it was the norm for children to be born at home. A room or a section of the house would be quarantined for the purpose and placed under the charge of traditional midwives who would assist with the delivery of the newborn. I was the second child to be born in that house after Sarla, my elder sister. Of my siblings, the eldest, Baijnath, and my next brother Narendra, died in their infancy.

I have only a few recollections of my father. He was a tall and strapping man with a moustache and would go to the stock exchange dressed in a dhoti and achkan in a carriage drawn by two horses. We also had an Adler, a German car quite popular among the well to do people of the time.

R.K. SOMANY

Though I didn't get much of an opportunity to interact with my father, I remember that Kakoji, as we called him, was very loving. Once every month, the entire family would sit together for a traditional Rajasthani meal of dal-bati-choorma. That was when he would talk to all of us. There was no dining table. We would sit on low stools and eat off silver thalis placed on small individual tables, or chaukis.

Kakoji was fond of wrestling, an activity he would indulge in three or four times a week for about an hour-and-a-half each. He was also very fond of horse racing—though he didn't own a horse—an unusual and rare hobby for Indians in those days. Kakoji, who hadn't been keeping well for several years, died at the Royal Calcutta Turf Club on 24 February 1944. I was not quite seven years old then. I recall his body being brought home in an open carriage, but I was too young to realize the import of what had happened. It was my sister Sarla's birthday.

My shocked reaction was: *'Kakoji to hai nahi. Kaun inaam dega after gilt cards?'* ('Father is no more. Who will reward my brothers for winning gilt cards?') Gilt cards were merit statements issued by St Xavier's Collegiate School, where my brothers Onkar Mal, Surendra Kumar and Chandra Kumar were studying, for good performance in individual subjects.

From that day, my eldest brother Hiralall, who was not yet 18 at the time and already married, became, for all practical purposes, my foster father, and his wife Kamla Bhabi, my foster mother. Most of what I have achieved in life is because of the guidance and support I have received from them. I have also received lots of affection and love from my second brother Onkar Bhaiji's wife, Ganga Bhabi.

Those must have been difficult times. We had a fairly large business, trading in raw jute and jute bags, moneylending, stock broking and export operations. The responsibility of running the business and bringing up eight younger siblings fell on Hiralall Bhaiji.

Some years earlier, he had dropped out of school to help Kakoji run the businesses. His schedule, following father's untimely death, became even more hectic, and he often worked for fifteen to sixteen hours a day. I hardly saw him; he would leave for work early in the morning and return late, so tired that he would often fall asleep without eating his dinner. Not once do I recall him complaining about the turn of events, though.

But I was too young to fully comprehend all that was going on. I had a comfortable, carefree childhood playing carom, cards, table tennis and flying kites. I remember my cousins (my maternal uncle's sons) coming over and playing with me on our huge terrace. The children of the Poddar family, our neighbours, would also come over regularly to play with us. Several members of the family have gone on to attain great success in business. Among them, Saroj Poddar is now chairman of the Adventz Group, as a part of the K.K. Birla Group has been renamed.

As the second youngest among a large brood of children, I often had to wait, and fight, for a chance to play. This instilled in me a fierce determination and fighting spirit that was to become a part of my character. My elder brothers and sisters tell me that I was an obedient, well-behaved child, not given to pranks. I, too, don't recall a single instance of any serious scolding or corporal punishment, a common feature in those days, being meted out to me.

At home, we spoke Marwari and Hindi and wore dhoti-kurta or kurta-pyjama. After me, no one in my family—neither my younger siblings nor any member of the next generation of the Somany clan—can speak proper Marwari, which is a pity because it signals a loss of touch with our native culture. At the same time, it also signifies a small step towards the homogenization of cultures across north India. It is a sign of the times. I don't know whether this is a welcome trend or not.

As was the custom of those times—which continues in many households across India—visiting family and friends would take off their shoes before entering our house. I couldn't stand the ugly sight of shoes, slippers and sandals lying scattered near the entrance. I would patiently stack them up, much to the everyone's surprise.

In those days, the atmosphere in many traditional families was very claustrophobic. Ours had a much broader outlook, without any choking orthodoxy. The women in our family also covered their heads but not fully, and my sisters-in-law would talk freely with my mother and grandmother.

When my brother Onkar Bhaiji got married, he and his wife started going to the movies together. This may seem quite commonplace now, but it was quite revolutionary for the time. We, including my sisters, would sometimes accompany them. But Onkar Bhaiji was very strict and I remember being quite scared of him. I enjoyed a much easier relationship Hiralall Bhaiji and his wife Kamla Bhabi, who took on much of the burden of running the household from my mother, a very kind-hearted and loving person.

I was particularly close to my sister Sarla, who studied at Loreto House, a leading convent school run by Irish nuns. I was also very close to Vinod Periwal, my *mama*'s (maternal uncle's) son, as well as Satish and Prem Biyani, who were the sons of my *bua* (father's sister).

A couple of private tutors would come home to give tuitions to my elder brothers and sisters. I, too, would sit down with them, which is how I picked up a rudimentary knowledge of English.

Kamla Bhabi would teach us Hindi and Sanskrit.

That was also the time I became an early riser. I shared a room with my brothers Surendra Kumar and Chandra Kumar, who were both older than I. As they had to wake up early to go to school, I too started waking up with them, thus, developing a routine that still continues seven-and-a-half decades later.

When it was my turn to start school, St Xavier's was the natural choice, as my older brothers, with the exception of Hiralall Bhaiji, also studied there, but more on that in the next chapter.

2

EDUCATION AND MY FORMATIVE YEARS

Very few men I know can claim to have studied in Loreto House, a venerable girls' school with a rich history and very successful alumni, located in Calcutta's Middleton Row.

When I was a little more than seven years old, Hiralall Bhaiji decided to enrol me in St Xavier's Collegiate School, a renowned Jesuit institution and one of Calcutta's most reputed boys' schools. It wasn't a difficult decision as my elder siblings Onkar Bhaiji, Surendra Kumar and Chandra Kumar all studied there.

In those days, gaining admission to the school wasn't as difficult as it is now. That three of my elder brothers were already studying there also helped my cause. But despite this, there was a small hitch. The school authorities said I could join only after three weeks. I don't remember why a three-week delay should have mattered so much, but in the interim I was admitted to Loreto House, which then took in a limited number of boys in the primary section. My elder sister Sarla was already a student there.

I attended classes at Loreto for all of three weeks, but that short period was enough to leave a lifelong mark on me. One day, I saw two of my classmates, both girls my age, throwing pebbles at each other. Unfortunately, their aim wasn't very good and a large pebble hit me full on my face, leaving a deep gash on my cheek. It healed soon, but I still carry a small scar on my right cheek to remind me of my short stint at Calcutta's premier girls' school.

Soon thereafter, I joined St Xavier's, which was to be alma mater for all my brothers except Hiralall Bhaiji. It was 1945.

St Xavier's, being one of two premier boys' schools in Calcutta then, had a very upper-class milieu. We had students from all communities in our class of about fifty students. A little less than half the boys were Bengali—mostly sons of barristers, bureaucrats, judges, landed gentry and businessmen. The rest, the non-Bengalis, came from every corner of India. Calcutta was then, along with Bombay, the biggest commercial centre in the country. It was home to the biggest Indian and foreign companies, or merchant companies, as they were called. So, it was natural that people from all over India migrated there for employment and livelihood. Marwaris made up the biggest contingent of this non-Bengali lot.

The atmosphere at school was, as a result, very cosmopolitan and I had friends from all communities. School life was fun, and we followed some quaint practices. Unlike today, we used to call each other by our surnames. For example, I was Somany to my friends. There was a fellow student called Baltiwala who studied with me for several years. I never learnt his first name. Also, we addressed boys we didn't know as 'Sonny'. For example, if one wanted to join a game with a group of boys one didn't know, it was common practice to approach one of them and say: 'Sonny, can I also play with you?' It was considered bad form to refuse. Lots of lifelong friends from St Xavier's first addressed their buddies as 'Sonny'.

I was a quiet boy, not given to aggressive behaviour, but two small incidents at school exposed a fierce side to my character and instilled in me a steely determination and will power that was to come in very handy throughout my life.

A Bengali boy called Bose would regularly complain to the teachers about me. He seemed to harbour a grudge against me for reasons I couldn't fathom. This carried on for almost three years. One day, after yet another unjustified complaint, I couldn't take it anymore. I went up to him during the lunch break and told him sharply: 'Look, Bose, I've had enough.' And slapped him!

Nobody intervened, not even his friends.

Bose complained to the Jesuit priest who was in charge of the primary school.

'What's going on, Somany?' the priest asked after summoning me to his office. 'Why did you slap Bose?'

All my pent up frustration came gushing forth and looking him straight in the eye, I blurted out: 'Father, he's been complaining about me without reason for more than three years. It's too much...'

The Father understood. He was silent for a few moments and then nodded. I slowly turned and left his office.

That incident changed my character. I had stood my ground on a principle and come away unscathed. Henceforth, I would never compromise over what I thought was right, whatever the cost. This little childhood incident has shaped my entire career. I was then in the fourth or the fifth standard.

The second incident that shaped my character occurred when I was in the ninth standard. There was a boy in class called Sanyal, much taller than I was, who would mockingly call some of us 'Mero'—a pejorative Bengali term for Marwaris. I found this irritating, but took it quietly.

We used to have an informal competition among ourselves. Boys had to 'bottoms up' a bottle of Coke, which cost 25 paise a bottle. If a boy failed to finish it in one go, he would have to pay.

Sanyal took up the challenge, failed, but refused to pay. To add insult to injury, he again sneered at us for being Mero.

This was not acceptable. He was much bigger than I and looked stronger. But I forgot all about Sanyal's relative physical advantage and hit him hard. We were on a balcony. His knee got caught between two bars in the railing and it took some effort to prise it out. He was in excruciating pain and had to be taken to the school infirmary for treatment.

Not surprisingly, he lodged a complaint against me, resulting in my having to visit the office of Father (later Cardinal) Lawrence Picachy, our prefect for discipline, who was much loved for his endearing ways as also equally feared for caning students who breached school discipline.

For the second time in four or five years, I looked a padre straight in the eye and said confidently: 'He went back on a commitment to pay. That's unacceptable. To top it, he sneeringly called me a Mero.'

Again, I was let off without punishment.

This must have rankled Sanyal, who had probably expected to see me being caned.

'Step out of school. We'll settle this score,' he said menacingly as we walked out of Father Picachy's ground-floor office.

'Why wait till then? Let's settle this right here,' I responded fiercely.

We glared at each other for a few seconds, pitting our wills against each other, neither of us willing to blink first, and then went our separate ways.

He never crossed me after that.

This reinforced my belief that I could stand up for my principles, against tough odds, and still win the day. This became the guiding principle of my life. More than a decade later, when I moved to Delhi to set up Hindusthan Twyfords (now HSIL), I found that dealers were demanding cash discounts for dues remitted six months after the due date.

'This is the practice here,' a big dealer once told me.

I was then in my mid-twenties and a novice in the business, having just entered the sanitaryware industry. I was also new to Delhi and didn't have any friends in the city. He was a veteran of the trade and thought perhaps he could bully me into submission. But it was a matter of principle. The steel embedded in my character all those years ago resurfaced. I minced no words in telling him that I would give cash discounts only for payments made within the scheduled date. The standoff didn't last too long. The dealer concerned, and others too, soon fell in line.

But coming back to my days at school, spare the rod and spoil the child was a popular saying when I was growing up. Corporal punishment was common at home and at school. St Xavier's had a well-earned reputation for imposing harsh physical punishment to enforce discipline. This was fairly common in most reputed boys' schools and I can't truthfully say that I came out any the worse from my experiences at the wrong end of a cane or a ruler. Parents, too, accepted this practice, so there was no backlash against it.

Typically, truant boys were asked to bend over and touch their toes. The teacher or the prefect for discipline would then administer two or three sharp raps on their buttocks with a three-foot-long cane. It was a painful experience designed to dissuade the recipient from repeating his offence. I'm not sure if the desired result was ever achieved, as many of my fellow students were habitual offenders.

Things are very different now. Social mores have changed dramatically over the last fifty years. Corporal punishment is now an offence that is punishable under the law. I personally have no views on either philosophy. It's just a sign of changing times.

As I have already mentioned, I was generally a mild-mannered, obedient boy. So, it came as a bit of a shock when I received my first 'bender'. I was then in the fourth standard. It was a hot and humid day and everyone was sweating profusely. A few beads of sweat fell on my exercise book, smudging the copy, written with a fountain pen. The class teacher was very upset. He hit me on the knuckles of my left hand with a cane. Although I soon forgot about the incident, I couldn't, at the time, figure out how sweating on a sultry summer afternoon could be a punishable offence.

My next 'appointment' with the wrong end of a cane came two years later, in the sixth standard. Our class teacher, Mr White, was a six-footer and weighed a hundred kilos. We didn't actually weigh him, but that was the consensus figure among students, based on his massive frame.

It was another hot summer day, and Narendra Thirani, a particularly naughty boy in my class, had earned the ire of Mr White. While I don't remember what Thirani had done, I clearly remember their exchange.

'Thirani, do you want to see stars in the daytime?' Mr White asked him.

As he looked uncomprehendingly at the towering giant, Mr White kicked his buttocks hard. Thirani didn't come to school for a week. If this had happened today, Mr White would have lost his job and gone to jail. It was an exceptionally brutal and uncivilized form of punishment even by the standards of the time. I do not know if Thirani's parents took the issue up with the school authorities, but Mr White seemed to carry on without a care in the world.

We were a class of fifty-five boys. All of us were scared of Mr White, but also resented his domineering ways. To get back at him, some of us came up with what we thought was a unique weapon. We got hold of a glass tube and devised a blow pipe through which we would fire chickpea pellets at Mr White when he turned towards the blackboard and had his back to us. This carried on for a few weeks, much to the irritation of our class teacher and the delight of the boys.

He would hector us, threaten us and cajole us to hand over the culprit(s) to him. I still feel proud that student solidarity held firm. Not one boy snitched on the 'shooters'.

It was too good to last. One day, I got caught—and found myself at the receiving end of Mr White's cane.

Let me add quickly that Mr White was the exception to the rule. The majority of our teachers were very good. In those days, most teachers in the primary section were women. Male teachers came into the picture from the sixth standard onwards. Most of them were Anglo-Indians who considered themselves British. There may have been a handful of Englishmen as well. They were very disciplined, and along with the Jesuit priests, taught me the importance of punctuality, correct behaviour, conduct, speech and etiquette. During lunchtime, some of them also taught us table manners, which was considered a very important part of a person's upbringing. These values have become an intrinsic part of my personality. Today, unfortunately, they are no longer considered as important as they once were and in my opinion, Indian society as a whole is the poorer for it.

Another very important facet of the Jesuit education I received was the centrality of morals. From the first standard till we graduated from school, we had one moral science class every week and a hundred mark test every term. The prescribed textbooks taught us morals of a secular nature and exhorted us to be good, caring human beings with a social conscience. This was a compulsory subject for all non-Christian students, who made up an overwhelming 85 to 90 per cent of the total student population at St Xavier's. I understand that this subject is no longer taught at schools. What a pity!

Unlike some other schools, we didn't have a school assembly every morning and would congregate in our classrooms at the start of the day and begin by reciting Christian prayers, mostly 'Our Father, who art in Heaven'. There was no compulsion for non-Christians to make the sign of the cross while reciting, 'In the name of the Father, Son, Holy Ghost, Amen,' and joining one's hands in prayer. But many of us did it out of habit.

We also wrote AMDG, the abbreviation for the Jesuit motto *Ad Majorem Dei Gloriam*', or 'For the greater glory of God', at the top of the first sheet of every test paper and class exercise. Not once did any priest or teacher make any attempt to convert a single student to Christianity.

The intense but friendly competition at school instilled in me a fierce desire to win and taught me the value of hard work. I was a little old for my class when I joined school. So, given my good overall performance, I was given a double promotion in the fourth standard. I told my second brother Onkar Bhaiji that I may not be able to cope, but he was cock-a-hoop over my academic excellence.

The euphoria was shortlived. I failed that year and had to repeat the class. This incident taught me that there are no shortcuts to success. It is said that failures are the pillars of our success. It is important for us to draw the right lessons from them and not get into a negative frame of mind and mope every time we stumble in our chosen path.

Though I was an average student overall, I did excel in a few subjects. I was good in English, geography, arithmetic and later, in the higher classes, in algebra and geometry as well. I remember being intensely disappointed when I failed to secure the first position in some subjects by a few marks. From the sixth standard onwards, I stepped up my efforts to do well in my studies. I was beginning to internalize another lesson that was to become second nature to me: there is no substitute for hard work.

It was around this time, in the sixth standard, that I made friendships that would stand the test of time and last me a lifetime. It was also the time that I became fluent in Bengali. Now, more than fifty years after I moved out of Calcutta, I can still converse in the language and friends tell me that I can still speak it like a native.

Nowadays, it is the norm to hire office assistants, earlier called peons, through outside agencies that specialize in providing these services. We follow this practice at HSIL. Many of the boys who work for us are Bengalis. Many of them claim to come from the West Bengal districts bordering Bangladesh. A few years ago, I overheard two of them talking about something. From their diction, I could tell that one of them was a Bangladeshi. I called him to my room and quizzed him in Hindi about his origins. He mentioned a border district. When I questioned him further, he even mentioned a village, with which I wasn't familiar. I then switched to Bengali and told him that his dialect betrayed his Bangladeshi origins. His eyes went wide with surprise. You could have knocked him over with a feather.

I try to catch a Bengali movie on television or on DVD most Sundays to stay in touch with the language. I particularly enjoy watching old black-and-white movies starring Uttam Kumar and Suchitra Sen.

As we progressed through the senior classes, everyone became more serious about studies. The board examination to mark the end of schooling was called School Final. I did fairly well, and secured a first division. My mother asked me: 'What can I give you as a reward?'

I said without hesitation: 'I want a Parker 51.' It was a big brand and soon, I was the proud owner of this coveted writing instrument. I treasured this pen for many years and wrote all my subsequent examinations with it. Sixty-three years later, I still have the pen.

I used to pride myself on my handwriting. Teachers would complement me on it and hold it up as an example for others to follow. 'Why can't you write like Somany?' was a common refrain. By the time I finished college, however, it had deteriorated. I blame the ballpoint pen for this fall in standards. Later in life, severe arthritis caused a further decline. My secretary Pooja now says she can't understand my scribbles.

It was now time for the next stage of my formal education. I decided to pursue commerce at the intermediate level (I. Com), corresponding to the current system of 'plus two' in St Xavier's. Many of my school friends, such as K.K. Kanoria, Om Rajgharia and Shri Mohan Jatia, all from well-known business families, dropped out of school to join their respective family businesses.

But I was determined to carry on with my studies. A few of my school friends—Anil Hirjee, who went on to become a barrister and managing director of Bombay Burmah Trading Company; Tarun

Das, who went on to become director general of the Confederation of Indian Industry; and Ajoy Mitra, whose father was a leading barrister—also enrolled for the intermediates at St Xavier's. Das opted for the science stream, Hirjee for arts and I chose commerce. I don't recall Mitra's choice of stream.

While pursuing I. Com, I began going to our office at 2 Red Cross Place in Calcutta's central business district where I learnt the basics of accounting.

It was also during those days that I first visited Darjeeling with my family. We rented a house called Sans Souci by the mall. It was bitterly cold. My job was to put coal in the boiler early every morning to heat the water.

Those were wonderful days. In the evenings, I would go to the skating rink with my brothers and sisters and learnt to skate. One day, we went to the races at the Lebong Race Course. I bet ₹10 on a horse and to my delight, won ₹150 when it beat all the favourites to finish first. It was a princely sum in the early 1950s. To celebrate, we had a party at Glenaries, the leading restaurant in Darjeeling, but I still had some money left over from my winnings.

We would return to Darjeeling every year for the next six to seven years for our annual family vacation and always stayed at Sans Souci. But I never again won a single race.

Back in Calcutta, I continued with my I. Com. The next two years passed by uneventfully. I completed the course, passing, once again, with a first division.

I wanted to continue my studies and was keen on pursuing a bachelor of commerce (B. Com) degree at St Xavier's, but my brother Onkar Bhaiji put his foot down.

'Why do you want to study? The business is growing and we need more hands on board,' he said. He and Chandra Kumar had quit studies after pursuing science at the intermediate level, while Surendra Kumar had done the same after completing his I. Com. Hiralall Bhaiji, as I've mentioned before, had not had the chance to complete his formal schooling.

I was in my late teens then, but I remember crying. I desperately wanted to study. For the first time in my life, I missed my father. Had he been alive, I wouldn't have been denied the chance of continuing with my studies, I thought.

Securing a B. Com degree was my Plan B, just in case I needed to turn professional and look for a job. I don't know why I felt this sense of insecurity. Our businesses were doing well and there was no dispute between us brothers. Nonetheless, I was determined to have a fallback option just in case I failed as a businessman. In those days, a university degree was enough to guarantee a well-paying job in any of the dozens of large companies and managing agencies that operated out of Calcutta.

Fortunately, B. Com classes at St Xavier's College were held from 6 a.m. to 9 a.m. This would allow me to pursue my education and also attend office. But I still had to fight every inch of the way to get what I wanted.

Onkar Bhaiji gave in reluctantly. 'I want you in office by 10 a.m. every day,' he said.

'I'll be there,' I replied confidently. Thus, I became the first member of the Somany clan to enrol for a college degree and three years later, the first Somany to graduate with a university degree. Unfortunately, I missed securing a first class by one solitary mark.

I had applied for three weeks of leave from work to prepare for the final university examinations. Hiralall Bhaiji granted me only two. But I had to return to work during this period of leave as an issue arose at one of our business concerns, R.B. Rodda &

Co, over some gun licenses. Since I was, by then, managing this part of the business almost independently, Hiralall Bhaiji wanted me to visit Lal Bazar, the Calcutta Police headquarters, to sort out the matter. As a result, I had only eight days to prepare for my exams. Though my family was happy with my results, I was intensely disappointed at missing out on a first class by such a small margin.

As I was pursuing my B. Com degree, I often felt there was so much to do and so little time to do it in. I had a packed schedule every day. College in the morning, a full day at office, French classes at Alliance Français three times a week and studying at night. How I wished the day could be extended by a few hours. But unknowingly, I was learning an important lesson that no college or formal system of education could teach: the art of time management.

Even now, nearing eighty, I work an average of sixteen to eighteen hours a day, juggling my time between my business, my commitments to the various committees of which I am a member, my doctors, physiotherapist and yoga teacher, and my family. I can say with all humility that I am very punctual and always read every relevant material carefully before arriving at meetings so that I can contribute meaningfully to the discussions that may take place. This would not be possible without efficient time management. And I learnt this art the hard way, while pursuing my B. Com degree.

Despite my packed schedule, Hirjee, Mitra and I still found the time to indulge in the typical fun things that youngsters do in college. Back then, I had a Chevrolet that I would drive to college. One day, we bunked classes and drove to Shriniwas, a reputed eatery near St Xavier's, for idli-sambhar. Unfortunately, our law teacher was also there gorging on his breakfast. He recognized my two fellow students and yanked us back to college.

'I don't recognize you,' he told me.

I smiled. I was learning the practical aspects of commercial law—which he taught—on the job at our office. So I had been skipping his lectures. Now, my transgressions had caught up with me. Fortunately, he didn't report us to the college authorities.

I was still in college when I began my lifelong love affair with guns. Hiralall Bhaiji had bought R.B. Rodda & Co, a gunsmith that imported rifles, shotguns, revolvers and ammunition. Hunting was still considered a sport for aristocrats. I had been working part time at Rodda and had developed a keen interest in guns.

One weekend, Hirjee, Mitra and I decided, on a whim, to visit the forests near Asansol, a few hours' drive from Calcutta, to hunt tigers. Mitra procured his father's hunting rifle, I managed to smuggle out a few rounds of ammunition and we were on our way in my Landmaster. I am a lifelong vegetarian and have never hunted an animal in my life. My exploits with guns are limited to shooting clay pigeons and target practice. But I was then just stepping into my twenties and the thought of going big-game hunting got my adrenaline pumping.

It was a hot summer afternoon. My car wasn't air conditioned and we were soon soaked with sweat, but we didn't mind. The adventure that lay ahead ensured we were agog with excitement.

Mitra's sister was married to a doctor in Asansol. We reached her house late that evening, ate a light meal and turned in early.

I had, a few months ago, installed a powerful spotlight on my car. It could be manoeuvred with the help of a lever attached inside car. We set out in the wee hours for the forest and for a fleeting moment, the spotlight caught a pair of bright green eyes we were sure belonged to a tiger. By the time Mitra had uncased his father's rifle, loaded it and was ready to fire, the eyes had vanished. We drove around for miles, but couldn't sight any other animal save for a few monkeys and birds.

Nonetheless, we were still excited. A tiger had only just managed to escape us. This was a tale that would make us heroes before our friends. But Mitra's brother-in-law, our host in Asansol, deflated our high spirits when we narrated our adventure to him.

'Tigers have amber eyes. The green eyes you saw probably belong to some other harmless animal,' he said.

We returned to Calcutta after resting for a while with our tails between our legs.

3

MY ELDEST BROTHER, MY LOCO PARENTIS

Kakoji, my father, died when I was barely seven years old, so I have very few memories of him. After he died, Hiralall, my eldest brother who I call Bhaiji, became, for all practical purposes, my foster father, guardian, mentor, guide and best friend all rolled into one.

He was all that and more, not only to me but to all of us siblings. It takes a rare human being to put his own education and possible future on the line to bring up his siblings. It takes an even more special person to provide for, and comfortably settle, eight younger siblings and still make a tremendous success of his own life.

Now, before I start sounding like a hagiographer, let me start at the beginning.

Kakoji, who had been adopted by my grandfather after his own son died, quickly established himself as a successful businessman and an able heir to Ram Prasad Somany. After grandfather's death, Kakoji expanded the family's jute trading, moneylending and stock-broking businesses, earning himself a solid reputation, both for his uncanny business acumen as well as for his probity.

In 1932, Kakoji suffered a heart attack. Bhaiji tells me that Kakoji suffered greatly. There were no painkillers in those days and when he was in pain, his cries could be heard more than 100 feet away.

He was never able to recover fully and, so Bhaiji had to leave school in 1936 to help Kakoji run the business. 'Kakoji told me he would not live much longer and that I should take over the business and look after my brothers and sisters,' Bhaiji told us many years later.

R.K. Bangur, a member of the venerable Bangur family, which was considered as being in the same league as the Birlas, Goenkas and Dalmias, was the doyen of the Calcutta Stock Exchange. When he heard that Bhaiji was Kakoji's son, it was enough for him. He admitted him as a member of the exchange solely on the strength of my father's reputation.

Bhaiji was still in his teens then but took to the stock-broking trade like a duck takes to water. 'I was a born speculator, took calculated risks and seldom lost money on my trades,' he would tell us later.

The Second World War broke out a few years after I was born in 1937. Calcutta was bombed by Japanese long-range bombers on the night of 20 December 1942, but the fear of aerial bombardment had been in the air ever since the start of the war.

Eight Japanese Ki-21 Type 97 bombers, which the British had codenamed Sally, bombed the city. Though an oil plant at Budge Budge, on the southeast fringes of the city, and the Calcutta Port seemed to have been the main targets, a bomb crater, possibly from a stray bomb, just outside the plush Great Eastern Hotel caused immense damage to morale.

The Japanese fighters returned four days later, on the night of 24 December 1942, just as Calcutta was getting into its traditional Christmas Eve festive spirit, and bombed the heart of central Calcutta, where most of the British establishments, offices and chic nightclubs were located.

Millions of people left the city in search of safety in the hinterland. Among them was my family. We travelled by bus to Dumka in neighbouring Bihar (Dumka is now in Jharkhand), which was a popular holiday destination for well-to-do Calcuttans. It is a beautiful place, with undulating terrain, jagged hills and rocky outcrops, and a salubrious climate except in summer. Many people still visit Dumka and its surrounding towns to recuperate from illness.

Kakoji's condition had worsened and our journey to Dumka was both an escape from possible Japanese bombing as well as a chance to give him an opportunity to regain his health. He had, by this time, disengaged himself almost entirely from the business, leaving Bhaiji in charge.

Our stay in Dumka was short, because soon after we arrived there, Kakoji expressed his wish to visit Chirawa, our native place in Rajasthan.

Kakoji's condition continued to deteriorate and he fell seriously ill. Water had gathered in his stomach and he was in great pain. There were no medical facilities in Chirawa, but Bhaiji managed to find a doctor willing to travel there to treat Kakoji. He administered an overdose of Salargon, a medicine made from mercury. Kakaoji then had to be administered glucose. He survived, but remained very weak. The doctor said his heart was in very poor condition. Bhaiji had, meanwhile, married Kamla Bhabi and she had insisted on accompanying us to Chirawa. Life was very difficult as sanitary facilities were rudimentary at best.

And Bhaiji was chafing at the bit. There wasn't much to do in Chirawa. The scare created by the Japanese bombing of Calcutta had ebbed and he longed to return to Calcutta. Kakoji needed urgent medical attention and the latest facilities to provide it. These were not available in Chirawa. And our businesses, the only means of sustaining a large family like ours, were being neglected.

So one day, Bhaiji had a massive showdown with Kakoji. Father was very angry but couldn't counter Bhaiji's logic for wanting to move back to Calcutta. He finally relented and we returned to our house on Ratu Sircar Lane.

We had left the business in the charge of our old munim (manager). My only recollection of the munim was that he had no teeth, which, for some reason, I found very amusing; I was not yet five years old.

We returned to Calcutta in 1941. World War II had been raging for more than two-and-a-half years. The prices of jute, hessian and sacks had risen dramatically and were fluctuating wildly. Our peers, who had stayed put in Calcutta, had amassed fortunes. We had missed out on part of the opportunity because of our long absence from the city. The munim had been able to manage just a holding operation.

Bhaiji, who had by this time gained the confidence of venerable business leaders such as G.D. Birla, Sir Badridas Goenka and R.K. Bangur, jumped into the fray with all his energy to make up for lost time. Within a few months, he wrested control of almost 99 per cent of the market for gunny in Karachi and some other parts of north-western India (Partition was still something only in the minds of the Muslim League and some British right-wingers).

We hardly saw Bhaiji at home as he would leave early every morning and return late at night. I remember him from those days as a tall young man dressed in dhoti-kurta rushing out to office every morning and returning home late in the evening. Occasionally, when he had to meet Europeans, he wore trousers and a shirt or sometimes, a suit.

'Because of heavy speculation, it was possible to earn profits of ₹10,000 to ₹30,000 per railway wagon of gunny, hessian and sacking sent to Karachi,' Bhaiji recounts. We were dispatching dozens of wagonloads every month.

The only problem was finding enough wagons. The primary task of the Indian Railways during this time was to supply war material to the troops on the front. Bhaiji was helped in his efforts to secure more wagons by one Mr Menessey, an Englishman with whom Bhaiji had developed a close association before the War. He looked upon Bhaiji as his own son and smoothed the way for obtaining allocations of the required wagons.

The prestige of the Somany family soared and we began to be counted among the leading trading families of Calcutta. But Bhaiji has a slightly different take on this. 'We never had money equivalent to our reputation,' he once said to me.

We were well off, but never as wealthy as some of the other leading Marwari families of Calcutta. But because Bhaiji had unfettered access to stalwarts like the Birlas, the Goenkas, the Jatias, the Bangurs and others, and they, in turn, showered their affection on him, many people thought we were much wealthier than we actually were. Bhaiji had also developed close ties with several stalwarts of the freedom movement, most notably with Sardar Vallabhbhai Patel.

Our stock-broking firm, which had its office at 7 Lyons Range, was also doing very well. Share prices were gyrating wildly during the war. Every day brought new developments. In 1942, the tide of the war was slowly turning in favour of the Allies. This brought in its wake new winners and losers on the stock exchange. Bhaiji, who was a born speculator, had an uncanny knack of picking winners, both in stocks as well as in jute, and the family businesses continued to prosper under his able guidance.

By this time, Kakoji had only a nominal presence in our business activities. As a result, Bhaiji realized there was a gap in his business education. He wasn't very proficient in accounting. Kakoji had always looked after this function, so Bhaiji had never felt the need to get too deeply involved. But the situation then demanded that he did, and so, he set about teaching himself the nuances of accounting with his usual grit and dedication, and soon mastered the art.

Despite earning lots of money in the jute trade, Bhaiji never thought of buying a jute mill, as many Marwari traders did in the years leading up to Independence and immediately thereafter. But he did make two unsuccessful attempts to enter the manufacturing sector in the 1940s, before finally meeting with success in the 1950s and 1960s in the ceramics and glass industries, in which the Somanys are now a household name.

Soon after returning from Chirawa, Bhaiji bought a tiny engineering unit called S.N. Ghosh & Company from a Bengali entrepreneur. It had its office at 16 Galif Street where it also ran a small workshop with one lathe machine and sixteen capstan machines with which it made tools for the Directorate General of Munitions Production.

My brother had no experience in the engineering industry.

'I saw a lathe machine for the first time after I bought the firm. Nevertheless, I taught myself how to use the lathe and the capstan machines and soon knew enough to be able to supervise my small team,' he later told me.

Bhaiji's next tryst with manufacturing came a year later in 1943. He set up Somany Glassworks in Belur, a small town near Calcutta, famous for the Belur Math set up by Swami Vivekananda as the headquarters of the Ramakrishna Mission. Here, he manufactured blown-glass items. The factory was still operational when the Second World War ended in 1945. But the technology employed was primitive and we didn't know how to control the heat required to make the glass. To make matters worse, the unit was beset with serious labour problems. We had no choice but to shut it down, but the experience Bhaiji gained in the art of management was to come in use when the family entered manufacturing in a big way a few years later.

Through all these years, while Bhaiji was making a name for himself and ensuring that the family had a comfortable life, the rest of us siblings were pursuing our studies while growing up in a typical Indian joint family. My grandmother was the unquestioned mistress of the house and she was assisted ably by Bhaiji's wife Kamla Bhabi, who, in addition to her household duties, also taught us Hindi and Sanskrit and sometimes helped out with our mathematics lessons.

Bhaiji was very approachable and warm with us on the rare occasions when he was able to spend some time at home and I developed a close bond with him, which is still intact. He would patiently answer all my childish questions, not admonishing me even once for raising what I'm sure, in hindsight, were pretty commonplace queries.

Several Indian business houses made huge fortunes during the

World War, after which, they invested this money in new businesses. In 1945, the British owners of R.B. Rodda & Company, one of India's biggest gunsmiths, were looking to sell out. The deal to buy the firm was offered to B.M. Birla, younger brother of G.D. Birla. B.M. Birla asked Bhaiji to buy the firm, which he did for about ₹4 lakh, a very large sum in those days.

Though labelled a gunmaker, R.B. Rodda & Co was in reality an importer of high-quality sports rifles, shotguns, revolvers, pistols and ammunition from leading European and American manufacturers.

The intervening years between the Second World War and Independence and Partition were fraught with political and communal tension and violence. Calcutta, in particular, bore the brunt of the savagery on 16 August 1946.

The Muslim League, which was propagating the division of British India into a Hindu-majority India and a Muslim-majority Pakistan, gave a call for a strike on that day in support of its demand. It was meant to be a show of strength and to display to the Congress, which had outright rejected its demand, as well as to the British rulers, the Muslim desire for a separate homeland.

The League named its call for a strike as 'Direct Action Day'. What followed was a communal conflagration of unimaginable proportions. More than 4,000 people lost their lives and over one lakh residents of Calcutta were rendered homeless.

R.B. Rodda & Co had the largest private armoury in eastern India. Bhaiji, as the owner, was a likely target, but he wasn't scared. I remember a well-dressed man coming home and collecting 2,000 rounds of ammunition from my brother. Bhaiji had earlier stored 5,000 rounds at home to be able to defend our family and neighbours if the need arose. Much later, I learnt that the man who came to Bhaiji was Amiya Nath Bose, a nephew of Netaji Subhash Chandra Bose and a senior leader of the Congress, who would later become India's ambassador to Burma.

Many years later, Bhaiji recounted his conversation with Bose. 'You look after the Marwaris. I'll look after the Bengalis,' Bose told him while collecting the ammunition.

Our house was close to a Muslim neighbourhood and though we were apolitical, this offered little security in those communally charged times. Some well-wishers had advised Bhaiji to evacuate us to a safer location, but he would have none of it. Right through the Great Calcutta Killings and Week of Long Knives, as the event came to be called, Bhaiji would patrol our house with a rifle slung over his shoulder and a revolver tucked into his belt. No one attacked our house or our neighbourhood.

I was barely nine years old then, but this display of raw courage in the face of the gravest physical danger etched itself in my mind and, perhaps unconsciously, became a template for my behavioural responses to adversity in later years.

Another incident from that time bears recording on these pages. A box of imported pistols, looted from the Customs shed at Calcutta Port, landed in Bhaiji's hands. He promptly gave them to G.D. Birla and Prabhu Dayal Himmatsingka, the famous freedom fighter, attorney and philanthropist.

Soon after Independence, Bhaiji recalls receiving an urgent summons from G.D. Birla, who was then in Simla. Upon reaching, he found Birla camped there with Sardar Patel and a few other Congress stalwarts. Patel was keen on integrating the then princely state of Hyderabad into India by armed action, but the Indian army was short of ammunition. Going through official channels would be time-consuming and Patel wasn't sure what the response of the western powers, where the ammunition factories were located, would be.

'Can you arrange it?' G.D. Birla asked Bhaiji. R.B. Rodda & Co had by this time become the largest private armoury in the country. We dealt only in sports guns. Military-grade ammunition was a different ballgame altogether.

It was a Herculean task. But Bhaiji had, by this time, developed deep contacts within ICI Ltd and other ammunition manufacturers in the West. He agreed. Since this issue involves national security, I have never asked Bhaiji for any further details and he hasn't revealed any to me, so this is all I know about the matter.

In 1951, Bhaiji decided to exit the jute business, which had been the mainstay of our family's good fortune. 'The milieu had turned dishonest,' he says. Several large jute traders with whom Bhaiji had dealings had diversified into industry in the years leading up to and immediately after Independence. They had been replaced by a new set of people who followed practices Bhaiji wasn't comfortable with. Thus, he left the business where he had cut his teeth in the world of commerce.

A few years later, in 1956, he also exited the stock market following a market crash that he had warned against.

Meanwhile, Bhaiji steered the family into its first successful industrial venture, setting up, along with my second brother Onkar Bhaiji, Hindusthan Glass Ltd in 1946.

B.M. Birla, who had encouraged Bhaiji to buy R.B. Rodda & Co in 1945, had taken Onkar Bhaiji with him to the United Kingdom in 1947 and pushed us to enter the glass business. We set up Hindusthan National Glass Manufacturing Co Ltd with a total investment of ₹25 lakh. The Birla family also put some money towards the company's capital.

Today, the company, managed by Chandra Kumar and his sons, is a market leader in the sector and makes bottles for several leading brands of beer and whisky and also makes the distinctively shaped bottles for Quink ink.

Thus, Bhaiji successfully made the transition from trading to manufacturing and helped each of us brothers set up industrial units that are all household names today.

4

INITIATION INTO BUSINESS

I have spent days at the Behala shooting range in Calcutta firing .375 magnum, .404 and .303 rifles, and imported hundreds of shotguns plated with gold and pistols with mother-of-pearl butts. I was custodian of a private armoury with 12 lakh rifle, shotgun and revolver rounds, one steel door and a key that had to be kept hidden in a secret location. And I still own three guns.

Does this conjure up images of the Wild West meeting a royal hunting party? Actually, these are only vignettes from my early career as a partner at R.B. Rodda & Co in the 1950s, when it was one of India's leading gunsmiths.

But I am getting ahead of myself. Let me start at the beginning.

My initiation into the world of commerce began almost as soon as I finished school in 1954. I began attending our office at 2 Red Cross Place even before I started attending I. Com classes at St Xavier's. It was drudge work initially—learning the traditional Marwari system of single-entry bookkeeping. This, Bhaiji and Onkar Bhaiji told me, was the very foundation on which the entire business edifice was built.

I would report for work every morning at the office of our jute-trading firm, Ram Prasad Muralidhar & Co, and patiently fill out page after page of transactions, trying to understand the nuances of cash flows, receivables and profits. Bhaiji and Onkar Bhaiji would keep a watchful eye on me and enquire every few weeks about my progress from our munim.

After about three months, Onkar Bhaiji, who was directly in charge of the business, declared himself satisfied with my progress. I then joined R.B. Rodda & Co, which had its showroom and workshop on the ground floor of the same building in which our jute-trading firm was located. Bhaiji and my third brother, Surendra Kumar, whom I call SK, were looking after this business, which, as you may recall, we had purchased a few years earlier on the recommendation of B.M. Birla.

Those were times when hunting, especially big-game hunting, was still considered a royal sport. I learnt the intricacies of the arms trade, importing sports rifles, shotguns, pistols, revolvers and ammunition from the leading manufacturers in the US, the UK and Germany.

R.B. Rodda & Co also had a second line of business—importing pumps, outboard motors, generator sets and diesel engines—which would, over the years, become even more important than its traditional arms business.

I took to both businesses like a duck to water. Since childhood, I had been keenly interested in all things mechanical. Like many children, I would strip my bicycle down to its constituent parts, wash them, grease them and reassemble the bike. As I grew older, I learnt to service my cousin's Lambretta scooter and even cars. Though I didn't have an engineering background, I had a natural affinity for tools and machines. Since both lines of business at R.B. Rodda were in areas I was keenly interested in, it was only natural that I would soon fall in love with my work.

However, I was unable to develop a liking for the jute-trading business, which had brought my family so much money and prestige, and in which Bhaiji and Onkar Bhaiji excelled. I couldn't master the trading game. I didn't enjoy working the phones through the day, placing buy and sell orders. But it was the mainstay of our business and couldn't be ignored. So, my involvement was limited to handling the accounts of the business. I am, perhaps, the only one among my brothers to never have bought and sold jute in my life.

Unlike at school, we didn't have classes through the day in I. Com. Often, there were just two classes a day. This gave me enough time to attend office regularly and gain valuable insights into how businesses are run.

Many hunters and sportsmen preferred rifles with mounted telescopic sights. Manufacturers in the West charged a large premium for guns with factory-fitted scopes. I imported a few Bruno rifles with mounted scopes, but they were very expensive. It was cheaper to import telescopic sights separately and mount them on guns locally. The margins on such sales were also much higher. So I began importing telescopic rifle sights mainly from Carl Zeiss of Germany. But fitting the scopes on rifles wasn't an easy task. It called for high-precision work on the rifle barrel. If you drilled even a millimetre more than necessary, you would weaken the barrel, exposing the shooter to danger. If you drilled less, the scope wouldn't hold steady for long, so accuracy would suffer.

I taught myself the intricate art of fitting rifles with telescopic sights. I even taught an assistant, a young Bengali man called Dhiren, how it was done. Thereafter, Rodda's margins increased and I was happy to have made my first major contribution to the family business.

Every Sunday, I would go to the shooting range in Behala on the outskirts of Calcutta and fire up to five hundred .22 rifle bullets at still targets. I would also shoot clay pigeons using a shotgun. Here, clay targets are fired into the air at varying speeds, elevations and angles from a machine called a trap. The shooter has to target these fast-moving flying objects. Essentially, the sport simulates live bird shooting, without actually putting any live birds in danger. The terminology of the sport, though, harks back to its violent origins in hunting. The inanimate target is still called a 'bird', a hit is called a 'kill' and a miss termed 'bird away'.

Soon, I gained a modicum of proficiency at this sport, and would spend hours on the range, shooting away at still and moving objects with a wide variety of rifles and shotguns. Those were fun days and I was learning something new every day. India had gained Independence just a few years before and princes, maharajahs, nawabs and kings still ruled the roost. Many of them were enthusiastic and skilled hunters. And being royalty, they often had special requirements. It wasn't an uncommon sight for a member of the Indian royalty to drive up to the doors of R.B. Rodda & Co in a Rolls Royce, Bentley, Cadillac or Minerva and order guns with their names or their family's coat of arms embossed in gold and silver. Small arms such as Webley & Scott and Smith & Wesson revolvers and Walther pistols with mother-of-pearl- or jewel-encrusted butts were also in great demand. I imported several such guns, many of them custom-made, from leading gunmakers in Europe and the United States for such royal customers.

C.K. Vissanji, who hailed from a wealthy business family with interests in the plywood industry, was then considered India's leading marksman. He telephoned one day to say he had some special requirements and asked if I could help him. Vissanji wanted a special Walther rifle and special cartridges that weren't available in India. I imported them for him and, over time, we became close friends.

But life wasn't all glamour and fun. Far from it! Red tape was already beginning to strangle and choke the business environment in India. I learnt the art of drafting official letters, and mastered the process of renewing licences, importing arms and ammunition and dealing with the Indian Ordnance Factory. Importing arms and ammunition, in particular, was a laborious process that required the filling up of numerous forms. I had to make multiple visits to the Customs office and other authorities for the necessary permits.

Those visits, boring at the time, taught me how to navigate the labyrinthine processes the government was putting in place and served as an important part of my education in business. The most important lesson I learnt was how to deal with the various arms and levels of the government.

Simultaneously, I was also cutting my teeth in the less glamorous side of R.B. Rodda's business. We had the agency to import Johnson outboard motors and GM Detroit diesel engines from the United States. We would sell these with generating systems or attach pumps to them and sell them to the Calcutta Water Supply Department, the municipal authorities and coal mines.

I learnt how to complete the necessary forms, negotiate rate contracts and conduct business with the Directorate General of Supplies & Disposals (DGS&D) under the ministry of commerce. We began supplying pumps with capacities of up to 1,000 HP and soon, the volume of business increased manifold.

R.B. Rodda was the first company in India to import submersible pumps from EMU in West Germany. These pumps had water-lubricated motors, a new technology in those days. When they burnt out, they required re-winding with special translucent plastic-coated copper wires that also had to be imported. The problem was there were few people in India who could do this. This was a high-margin business and we didn't want to lose it. So I taught myself how to wind these wires in the Rodda workshop.

The starters for these pumps were also very expensive and difficult to procure, so many users would compromise and user cheaper, locally available alternatives. This led to frequent malfunctions, resulting in the motors burning out. Nobody could do the winding that was needed to get these machines back in operation. Once again, I learnt how to re-wind these pumps. That meant mastering the number of rounds that were required and procuring the special tools needed for the operation. Soon, I learnt the art of repairing these machines, began importing starters and serviced hundreds of such pumps. Thereafter, this business became very successful.

We had an engineer named Ghosh, who we once despatched to Asansol, an industrial town near Calcutta, to repair a GM Detroit six-cylinder diesel engine. He called me after three days—via trunk call, as direct dialling was still a few years away—to say that he hadn't been able to fix the engine despite his best efforts.

I travelled by train to Asansol, booked myself into a small, ramshackle hotel and proceeded to the client's factory. Ghosh and our client had probably expected me to only supervise the repair of the malfunctioning engine. Their eyes almost popped out when they saw me change into a workman's overalls and proceed to personally dismantle the engine, diagnose the problem, set it right, clean and grease individual parts and then reassemble the machine. By the end of it, I was covered in grease and grime, but I felt satisfied. This was the first time I had actually dirtied my hands at a client's site, although I had regularly been repairing machines at our workshop behind the R.B. Rodda & Co showroom.

As I spent time at Rodda, I grew more confident of my abilities and began to think of ways to expand the business. I ramped up the import of cartridges. Towards the end of my tenure at Rodda, I was importing 15 lakh cartridges every year—by far the highest number by any private firm at that time—mainly from the UK-based ICI Ltd. I set up a strongroom to store this massive amount of ordnance.

There were strict rules governing the setting up of ammunition strongrooms. The smallest spark could set off a catastrophic explosion of diabolical proportions. The slightest patch of damp could render a massive cache of ammunition completely useless. And there was the constant fear that elements inimical to the state and to public order would try to lay their hands on the destructive power that lay within the vault. For security reasons, the strongroom had only one entrance. We had to keep the keys hidden and only a few family members knew where they were kept. Fortunately, the armoury remained safe and nothing untoward happened.

By this time, we were making annual profits of ₹10 lakh from the sale of cartridges alone. It was a humungous amount in the 1950s, worth several kings' ransoms. I can, with some satisfaction, take credit for having expanded Rodda's business manifold in the years before I left for Delhi.

In 1947, B.M. Birla, the man behind Hindustan Motors, India's first passenger-car company, took Onkar Bhaiji with him to the

United Kingdom. Onkar Bhaiji's wife, Ganga Bhabi, was B.M. Birla's daughter and G.P. Birla's sister. They had married in 1943. As I have mentioned earlier, B.M. Birla had prompted Bhaiji to buy R.B. Rodda. Now, he pushed us to enter the glass business.

With his active encouragement and under Bhaiji's leadership, the family set up Hindusthan National Glass & Industries in 1954 with an investment was ₹25 lakh, a massive sum of money in those days. The Birlas also invested some money in this venture.

The company, now under the management and control of my fourth brother Chandra Kumar, makes bottles for a wide variety of industries such as pharmaceuticals, liquor, cosmetics, food products and consumer goods. Its clients include such household names as Coca Cola, ITC, Nestle, Ranbaxy, Diageo, Dabur, Hindustan Unilever, among many others.

In 1957, under the guidance of Bhaiji and Onkar Bhaiji, I started considering various options for entering the manufacturing sector. We zeroed in on the sanitaryware sector. From 1959, I began to study the workings and requirements of the sector. We decided to go in for vitreous china, a new technology at the time. It was different from regular earthenware china products because it didn't absorb water even if the product chipped. No other company was making it in India. People told us it was a mistake, that the product would be expensive for a country like India and that the technology hadn't yet been tried out in a country such as ours. Instead, they advised, we should go in for regular china products.

It was again a matter of principle. Lessons learnt early in life had shown me that compromises on quality only led to mediocre products and sub-optimal outcomes. Bhaiji, Onkar Bhaiji and I were determined to go in for the latest technology and provide Indian consumers with the best products available.

After scouting around the world, we settled on Twyfords Ltd, an English firm that was one of the global leaders in sanitaryware, as our partner. Twyfords had been in business for more than 200 years—since 1758. J.R.T. 'Jack' Hay, the chairman of Twyfords, was willing to share his company's technology with us and after a few rounds of discussions, we signed an agreement.

'The production process in the sanitaryware industry needs close supervision. You should nominate a family member to visit England and train with us for a few months,' Jack told Bhaiji. By then, Onkar Bhaiji and Chandra Kumar were already involved with Hindusthan National Glass and Surendra Kumar with Simplex Mills. I was the only family member available. So it was that I entered the ceramics industry, of which I knew nothing.

It is interesting that from very early times, my family has entered new sectors in which it had no experience and emerged successful. As I've mentioned earlier, my grandfather left behind a thriving moneylending business in Chirawa, Rajasthan, migrated to Calcutta in the early years of the twentieth century and established himself in the jute business, becoming, over time, the largest trader of jute in north-western India (which later became Pakistan).

A few years later, he and my father set up a stock broking firm, which added to the family's wealth and prestige. Bhaiji carried on this tradition of risk-taking and entrepreneurship, acquiring R.B. Rodda & Co, which we expanded into India's biggest gunsmith and ammunition importer, as well as eastern India's largest importer of American and European engines, pumps and outboard motors. Then, despite two failed attempts at entering the manufacturing sector, Bhaiji successfully shepherded Onkar Bhaiji, Chandra Kumar, Surendra Kumar and me into manufacturing.

I had married Krishna Mohta in 1959, after graduating from

St Xavier's College the year before. And soon after, when the partnership with Twyfords was struck, Krishna and I left for the UK so I could undergo training at the firm. We flew to Switzerland, spent ten wonderful days touring the country, and then flew to London. After spending two days in the British capital seeing the sights, we proceeded to Stoke-on-Trent in Staffordshire, the heart of the ceramics industry.

Jack Hay assigned the responsibility of training me to N.R. 'Reg' Hancock, a senior executive on the technical side of the company. Reg, a very warm and affectionate man, had a formidable reputation in the ceramics industry. We took an instant liking to each other and he took Krishna and me under his wing.

Three other executives from HTL—V.S. Bhatt, a technical man, M.N. Bhave, a modeller, and P.B. Shetty, a slip and mill house specialist—were also sent to England for training. So, in addition to receiving training myself, I had the responsibility of keeping track of their progress. A decade-and-a-half later, when one of them betrayed me at the instigation of one of my own siblings, I had occasion to reflect on the effort I had invested on his training in England.

I began my training at Twyfords within a day or two of arriving at Stoke-on-Trent. Jack Hay, who addressed me as 'Number Five', since I was the fifth brother, called me to his chamber on the first day and explained my duties to me. He also very graciously invited me to dine with the directors in the luncheon room reserved for the top management of the company.

The training was rigorous, thorough and often physically taxing. Reg had drawn up a detailed programme to guide me through the entire process of making ceramic products.

The first step was learning how to make Plaster-of-Paris moulds for the sanitaryware that was to be created. It took me two months to learn this art, which is the very foundation of the ceramics industry.

The casts were very heavy and the job called for considerable physical strength. I'm a slightly built person and the chronic medical issues I faced later in life with my right arm probably had their genesis in my exertions during those months spent in a ceramics factory in England.

Up to a few years earlier, during 1956–58 while I was still in college, I would go to the office of our stock-broking firm every Monday, Tuesday and Wednesday and sign up to 500 cheques a day. A year-and-a-half later, that is, after my stint in Twyfords' casting unit, my arm had begun to give me so much trouble that I began to avoid writing as much as I could. But despite the pain and the acute discomfort I faced, and continue to face, I have no complaints. I was learning new things every day and I owe a lot of my success in the ceramics industry to those physically taxing, but otherwise enjoyable, days spent learning the ropes in England.

After casting, I learnt the art and science of glazing and worked in the kilns for two weeks. Thereafter, I spent time in the Twyfords laboratories and finished my training in the slip and mill houses.

Thus, I learnt the intricacies of making ceramics on the shop floor. It was an education no university degree could have replicated. Since I was working with products that would soon be shipped out to dealers across the United Kingdom and the world, I learnt all the trade secrets that veteran ceramic experts employed to get around the many problems that invariably crop up on every factory floor.

Jack would often drop in unannounced to check how I was doing. I remember feeling a sense of déjà vu—recalling my early days in business under the watchful eyes of Bhaiji and Onkar Bhaiji—when Jack would enquire about my progress.

My training in England lasted five-and-a-half months. I would leave for the factory and/or office early every morning and return home by evening. But it wasn't all work and no play, for unlike the proverbial Jack, I had no intentions of becoming a dull boy.

As I mentioned earlier, Jack had invited me to dine with the directors. When I told him that I was vegetarian, he made it a point to ensure that I was served mashed potatos, some vegetables, bread, soup, butter and some sweets. In my honour, he even had a small Indian flag placed next to the Union Jack that was kept in the luncheon room. One day, I saw that the Tricolour was flying upside down.

'May I point out a mistake?' I asked Jack politely.

On learning the cause of my discomfort, he immediately had the mistake rectified.

It wasn't just Jack who looked after my wife and me. The entire top management of Twyfords—from Jack and his wife Mary to Reg and his wife Dorothy and several others—went out of their way to make us feel at home. Every weekend, Jack, Reg or one of the other directors would invite us home or take us out.

The hospitality of my British colleagues, however, presented an unexpected problem for us. Supper, for the English then, was served at 6 p.m., which was barely past our tea time. But it would be rude to turn down their hospitality. So, Krishna and I would return home and eat an apple each at our regular dinner time a couple of hours later.

Another Twyfords colleague whose hospitality I remember vividly is F.C. Puckridge, the company's marketing director. He and his French wife were excellent hosts and I still recall the delicious food they would serve. Vegetarian food wasn't very popular or easily available in England those days; I wish to take this opportunity to put on record my sincere appreciation for the efforts they took to accommodate our food habits.

Jack and Mary were particularly warm and welcoming and Krishna and I spent many a wonderful evening at their beautiful house enjoying their hospitality. As is the norm in Europe, the Hays didn't have any domestic help. So Krishna would help Mary clear up and wash the dishes after we ate. I still remember one evening, when Mary and Krishna had carried the plates into the kitchen, Jack asked me a little sheepishly: 'RK, pass me the chocolate pudding... err...and don't tell Mary.' He had gout and diabetes and had been forbidden by his doctor from consuming sweets, but couldn't resist the temptation of sometimes tucking into his favourite dessert on the sly. Krishna chuckled loudly when I recounted this episode to her later that evening.

We, too, returned their hospitality by inviting them over to our rented apartment. We would usually serve rice, puris, a dal and some Indian vegetables. Krishna was a very good cook and the aroma of the food would waft out from the kitchen, whetting our appetites.

'Look at the quality of rice,' gushed Jack on one occasion. Basmati, now so common at neighbourhood stores across the length and breadth of the United Kingdom—and indeed, many other countries—was still a rarity on English shelves. We had carried several packets of this aromatic long-grained rice with us for our own consumption. I told Krishna to give one to Mary.

The previous year, Alex Joshua Miller, the technical director of Twyfords, had visited India when negotiations on our proposed joint venture were in progress. During dinner at our house one day—quite possibly his first exposure to Indian vegetarian cuisine—he seemed intrigued by the shape of the puris we had served. After dinner, he took me aside and asked: 'Somany, how do you put compressed air into puris?'

Indian cuisine was not very popular in England those days, so his innocent question was, perhaps, not entirely unexpected. Since the 1980s, however, Indian food has become tremendously popular in England and there are hundreds of Indian restaurants in London and other British cities run mostly by Sylheti cooks from Bangladesh or chefs from Pakistan's Baltistan region. I'm told that rice and curry, that quintessential Indian staple meal, is the food of choice in many British households and that chicken tikka masala is not an Indian dish at all.

'Chicken tikka masala is now a true British national dish, not only because it is the most popular, but because it is a perfect illustration of the way Britain absorbs and adapts external influences,' British foreign secretary Robin Cook said about a decade-and-a-half ago.

Being vegetarian, I have no comments on the merits of Mr Cook's assertion except to note how times have changed since my first visit to England almost six decades ago.

Both Krishna and I had led fairly sheltered lives in Calcutta and though neither family was ostentatious, we had never had to personally attend to daily chores such as cooking, shopping for groceries, dusting or doing the laundry. Also, though both of us were very careful in our spending habits, living on five pounds a day, which was what I was entitled to carry in those days of foreign exchange controls, wasn't easy.

It was, thus, a learning experience for us when we rented an apartment at 27 Woodlands Avenue in Stoke-on-Trent. The grocery store was about 500 metres away. Krishna would often walk across to buy whatever we needed. I would sometimes accompany her.

The furnished flat came with a black-and-white television—a novelty for Indians those days. Television would come to Calcutta more than a decade-and-a-half later. There was no Indian programming those days, but Krishna and I spent many an enjoyable evening watching English programmes while lounging in front of the television set.

As was the norm in those days, Krishna and I hadn't gone through a period of courtship, and we had moved to England soon after our marriage. So the five-and-a-half months we spent in England served as an extended honeymoon and turned us from mere spouses into best friends.

Once, when I had a long weekend off from work, Krishna and I drove across to Paris, crossing the English Channel on a ferry. We spent a wonderful few days driving around the French countryside, soaking up the atmosphere. I realized sometime during the trip that my car was low on engine oil.

'Do you have Mobil?' I asked at the next petrol pump I stopped at.

'No,' came the short and crisp answer.

This scene repeated itself at more than twenty petrol pumps. I was getting desperate, but somehow managed to coax my Austin 7 back to Stoke-on-Trent. It was much later that I learnt why French petrol pumps had been unable to provide me with engine oil. In India, Mobil had become the generic name for this class of lubricants as it was the only brand available. Out of habit, I had asked for Mobil instead of 'engine oil', and the attendants, assuming that I wanted that specific brand, had not offered any alternative.

One last incident that I would like to share with readers pertains to my return. One of my brothers informed me that the Customs rules for returning Indians were being changed with effect from 1

September 1961. The value of items people could bring in without paying customs duty would be considerably reduced from that day. So I advanced my plans and touched down in Calcutta on 31 August, beating the deadline by only a few hours.

Krishna had bought a lovely Wedgewood crockery set for thirty people. The world leader in bone china crockery had even given me a handsome discount on Jack's recommendation. Despite this, its value would have taken my belongings beyond the permissible threshold. But I needn't have worried. The ever-resourceful Jack arranged to have it delivered to me by a member of a British delegation that visited India shortly afterwards.

By the end of my training period, I had learnt a lot more than just how to make ceramics. For one, my wife had become my best friend—a very important thing, especially as we would spend the next decade and more as a nuclear family in Delhi, where we had no family and friends. For another, we had learnt how to make every pound stretch that extra bit as we tried to live to the best of our abilities within a limited income. This enforced thrift taught both of us the importance of the saying 'a penny saved is a penny earned'. And finally, it taught us how to live independently in a strange land where we had to resolve the day-to-day issues that invariably crop up in the course of life.

Within a week of returning to Calcutta after completing my training, we moved again, this time to Delhi, which became my home for the rest of my life. The experience gained and the lessons learnt in the six months I spent abroad were invaluable in helping us settle down in the capital. Soon, I would get involved with the setting up and running of the newly incorporated Hindusthan Twyfords Ltd (later Hindustan Sanitaryware and now, HSIL).

As I have mentioned in the previous pages, Bhaiji had shut down our jute-trading and stock-broking firms as the family began to take its first baby steps in the world of manufacturing. But R.B. Rodda & Co, where I had apprenticed and where I learnt the nuts and bolts of business, is still with the Somany clan. After an amicable division of the family's assets in the 1990s, the company, which still exists, albeit as a dormant one, went to my brother Surendra Kumar. Although the rest of the family no longer has anything to do with it, I still retain my emotional bonds with the company that gave me and my family so much.

5

MY HOBBIES AND INTERESTS

Let me begin this chapter with a full disclosure. I got my driver's licence on 9 September 1951, a few months before my fourteenth birthday—more than four years before reaching the age prescribed by the law. That licence was rightly cancelled when I was found out, but so many decades later, I still remember the number—36661.

I had been interested in cars and other machines from an early age, but I got my driving licence courtesy my brothers' passion for bridge. Bhaiji, Surendra Kumar and Chandra Kumar were keen bridge players. So was an uncle and a brother-in-law. Every weekend, they would go over to my brother-in-law's house to indulge in their love for this card game.

Like many young children, I would sit behind the wheel of our car, the key in the ignition, press the starter and kick the engine to life. I would then rev the engine of the stationary car and pretend I was driving down a road at high speed. This is a fantasy that millions of young children have played out in their garages and driveways.

Soon, I graduated to working the clutch and putting the car into motion—in first gear and reverse, moving only a few yards in each direction—tentatively to begin with and then more confidently as I slowly mastered the coordination required between my eyes, mind, hands and feet.

We had three cars, but only one driver. One of the cars was a Studebaker. It was a big American car capable of great pick-up and speed and I loved driving it.

My brothers found out what I was up to, but fortunately, accepted it as natural for a growing child. A few months later, I was ferrying my brothers home from my brother-in-law's house and dropping my uncle back to his house after his visits to our home. These transgressions of the law were always on Sundays when there were hardly any policemen on the streets, so I got away with it.

I was finally caught out when I was preparing to go to England almost a decade later. When I applied for an international driving licence, the discrepancy between the age on my passport and my driving licence gave my game away.

Fortunately, I wasn't penalized. All I had to do was take a driving test and apply for a new licence. But the experience taught me a lesson: never breach the law. It's a lesson I've internalized and followed scrupulously all my life.

I have never remotely considered studying engineering but have, from as long as I can remember, taken a keen interest in all things mechanical. Playing with screwdrivers, pliers and gauges gave me great pleasure in my childhood and as I grew older, my amateur attempts at playing engineer became a passion.

BRINGING THE RAINBOW

I must have been about ten or eleven years old. Bhaiji told me: 'If you get 90 per cent marks, I'll give you anything you want.' I immediately asked for a Mechano set and spent hours making cranes, lorries and the more complicated designs from the book that came with the Mechano set. For my class exhibition, I made an Eiffel Tower with a lift that could go up and down by means of an electric motor using various reduction gears.

When Onkar Bhaiji went to the United States, he got his son Shashi a Lionel miniature train set and an EDB airplane. Shashi was only six or seven years old and couldn't set up the system. He asked all the elders, but everyone was busy with their own chores.

I was about twelve years old at the time.

He asked me: 'Chachaji, will you help me set it up?'

I gladly agreed to help him. It was a pretty complex system, with towers, signals, junctions and crossings and took a few days to set up. But it was worth the effort, and I learnt a lot from the exercise.

My passion also exposed me to a fair bit of danger. In the years immediately after Independence, the spirit of patriotism that had won us freedom was still running high. Many families lit up their houses to celebrate Independence Day and other important national occasions.

It was 25 January 1950, a day before our country was to become a republic and cut the last vestiges of the political ties that still bound us to our former rulers. We were then living in a rented house on 13 Store Road (now called Gurusaday Road). Night had fallen—it was around 10 p.m. Wearing a set of khadau (the wooden slippers typically worn by sadhus), I was stringing up lights throughout the house to celebrate our first Republic Day. I don't recall why I stepped out of the khadau, which were serving as an insulator, but while working on the lights, I touched the naked end of a 35-foot long wire I had connected to an electrical outlet inside the house.

A bolt of shock ran through me and I fainted, still clutching the wire. Fortunately, my sister's brother-in-law was close by. Showing great presence of mind, he yanked the wire out of the plug point, thus, saving my life. I was unconscious for a couple of hours. The live wire left a six-millimetre hole on the index finger of my left hand. I still have a scar to remind me of that day when I almost died.

But this accident and the near-death experience did not in any way diminish my curiosity or love for machines and engineering. My mother would often ask me to take a look at a regulator, or a lamp, or a fan in her room that wasn't working. I would then fix the malfunctioning machine. My mother and the rest of the family soon came to rely on me to repair things around the house.

As the owners of R.B. Rodda & Co, it was but natural and there would be guns in our house. From a very young age, I developed my skills as a marksman using my brothers' airgun. I would also oil and clean their guns. In the process, I learnt how to dismantle and assemble various kinds of rifles, shotguns, revolvers and pistols. When I was legally able to own my own guns, I would go to the Behala shooting range to hone my skills as a marksman.

My interest in machines was to earn my family and me a lot of money. I have mentioned earlier how I took charge of all the mechanical and engineering functions at R.B. Rodda & Co, fixing telescopic sights on rifles, repairing water lubricated and other pumps and all the various kinds of motors and engines we were importing.

Behind the R.B. Rodda & Co showroom at 2 Red Cross

Place, we had a small workshop with vices, lathes, pipe threading tools and a host of other implements required for repairing guns and machines. Here, I learnt how to connect plugs to switches, understood the concept of negative, positive and neutral, and learnt how to protect myself from shocks.

Soon, I began repairing our cars. In the mid-1950s, we had a Chevrolet, which had been giving trouble. I took out the engine block, re-bored the chambers and changed the pistons of the six-cylinder engine. I can't describe the pleasure I felt when, after my efforts, the engine purred to life. I immediately drove the car to Diamond Harbour Road, then a deserted highway leading out of Calcutta, and stepped on the gas. The speedometer touched 100 mph and the wind brushed against my face. It was exhilarating.

I got my first brand-new cycle when I was well into my teens. All the cycles I had had previously were hand-me-downs from my brothers. Onkar Bhaiji told me: 'If you reach this level (he set a minimum threshold) in your studies, I'll give you whatever you want.'

I asked for a Raleigh cycle. Three-speed gears had just been introduced and I wanted a set for my cycle. It cost ₹200-300. My brother refused my request. So, I bought a set as well as a dynamo with my own money and fitted them myself.

I remember taking the cycle to Ranchi where we had a farmhouse not far from the Birla mansion. I rode 20 to 30 kilometres every day. One day, I dismantled the entire gear mechanism to see how it worked. I would also service the cycle myself.

I remember being asked by two of my nephews and a first cousin to teach them how to overhaul a car engine. A Rover 80 was giving trouble. The mechanic couldn't figure out which tepid was causing the problem. I jumped in, and not only repaired the problem component, but also did the valve setting, flushed the radiator and changed the engine oil. All this while, my 'students' were watching all this from a safe distance while I was getting my hands dirty—literally. Once, my finger almost got chopped off when it got caught in a radiator fan, but I shrugged it off as the price of learning something new.

This taught me another important lesson. To be successful, one has to be in the thick of the action. Observing others from a distance and barking out orders serves the purpose only up to a point. But unless you know the nuts and bolts of the issue at hand—I believe the popular term for it in modern management-speak is 'going granular'—you will always be at the mercy of others who may or may not be able to deliver the results you want.

My brother Surendra Kumar had moved to Bombay in 1958 to help run Simplex Textiles, which belonged to his father-in-law. We had bought a large stake in the company and had become partners. In September that year, it was decided that our Morris 8 would be sent to him.

I remember being woken up early one morning. The Morris 8, which was scheduled to leave for Bombay by road, wasn't starting. I got down to work and fixed the problem. But a spanner slipped and hit my index finger, slicing it open and exposing the bone. An alarm was raised and my mother came running out. She fainted at the sight of so much blood.

In spite of my injury, it gave me great satisfaction that the car made the journey of almost 2,000 km without once breaking down.

I have worked on a wide variety of cars and engines and can say with confidence that if anyone gives me an old jalopy, the necessary tools and a spare tyre, I can drive that car anywhere.

Now, one no longer needs to tune car engines manually.

Everything is computerized. Service-centre workers simply hook the engine to a computer, which takes care of everything. This is a more efficient way of doing things, but it has taken the romance out of car maintenance.

Back in the 1950s, it was difficult to find spare parts for cars. Windshield wipers would wear out with use, but replacements weren't always available. Calcutta receives very heavy rainfall from mid-April to the end of September and sometimes beyond. Blinding sheets of water would pour down from the heavens, reducing visibility while driving. Not having windshield wipers is very dangerous in such situations. Through a process of trial and error, I found a way to cope with the rains even without them. Rub raw onions on the windshield of your car if the wipers stop working. The water will simply run off, giving you a reasonably good sight of the road ahead.

I used to drive quite regularly till my seventy-eighth birthday but a chronic problem with my right shoulder has forced me to curtail my driving. It isn't the steering wheel that bothers me as much as opening and closing the big and heavy doors of my Mercedes Benz. I also own a Bentley, a Lambhorgini and a Ferrari, but it is my son Sandip who mainly drives these high-performance cars.

My interest in engineering saved the day for my business on several occasions. I have already recounted the story of how I fixed a malfunctioning engine in Asansol. On another occasion, I entered a hot kiln in our Bahadurgarh plant and repaired it. One more such incident bears recalling here. In 1963, the HTL plant was ready and we were scheduled to officially start operations soon. At 7 p.m. on the day before we were to commence commercial production, an imported crane that was critical to our operations broke down.

Reg Hancock, who had been deputed to HTL to assist with

the technical side of things, said we would have to defer the official start of our operations till the crane was fixed. That could take weeks as technicians would have to fly in from England. As the following day was an auspicious one, I didn't want any delays. When Reg went to his room for coffee, I told my workers to rig out a bamboo hoist and climbed up the crane.

Reg was horrified when he returned. 'RK, what are you doing? You'll die if you fall,' he screamed.

I told him that I would have to die some day. "Let me finish my work and get the crane restarted." I had, in that time, discovered the problem. A brake shoe had got locked and was preventing the crane from working. I unscrewed the shoe and refitted it. The crane was back in working order. We saved a packet by not having to send for foreign technicians and the official launch of our operations went ahead as scheduled the next day. Reg was amazed.

I'm certain there are many such unrecorded incidents of native intelligence and ingenuity across Indian industry. Indians have been practising frugal engineering from much before the term gained global currency.

Given my interest in and passion for all things mechanical, it is perhaps natural that I have collected a large variety of tools for my personal use. I have almost a hundred different types of screwdrivers. Till recently, I would repair the electrical appliances in my house myself. Once, when a fan in my house wasn't working, I fetched a ladder, climbed up and was fixing the fan when my elder daughter walked into the room. She was both concerned and horrified. 'You can injure yourself very seriously if you fall, Papa,' she said.

'The electrician was taking his time coming, so I decided to do it myself,' I replied and carried on with the repairs.

On another occasion, a carpenter had demanded ₹15,000 to open eight crates of furniture that I had bought for my house in Hyderabad. I told my guard to buy a hammer with a hook and opened the crates myself.

Apart from guns and mechanical toys, I love reading. In my youth, I loved detective novels and thrillers. Agatha Christie and Earl Stanley Gardener were my favourites. I enjoyed the way these masters of crime writing would build up their plots, casting equal suspicion on each of a large cast of characters before unveiling the criminal with precision logic.

As I grew older, my reading habits changed. Now, apart from technical journals, I enjoy reading biographies—especially of successful business leaders—to try and learn something from their experiences.

I was an avid stamp collector, a popular hobby among youngsters of my time. We had a class teacher at school, Father Vanbynder, who also collected stamps. He would call me to his room after class and tell me about philately. We also exchanged a few stamps. I still have some of my albums, though I'm no longer active in increasing my collection, most of which is with my nephew, who took it over when I left Calcutta, first for England and then for Delhi in the early 1960s. And I've misplaced a large part of what was left with me, probably while moving houses.

Even now, I try to teach myself something new every few days. The challenge of picking up new skills and knowledge keeps me alive and fresh and also keeps me in tune with the times. I hope I can maintain this habit till the very end.

6

TAKING A RISK: A NEW BEGINNING

Our haveli in Chirawa was large, in line with our status as one of the prominent families in the area. But like many others, we had no toilet within the premises. We had to go out behind the bushes and shrubs to relieve ourselves. I do not know why this was so. Perhaps it had to do with concepts of hygiene prevalent at the time. Nonetheless, it was inconvenient and dangerous, especially for women. Fortunately, in those days, heinous sexual crimes against women were rare—and unheard of in Chirawa. But rattlesnakes, scorpions, and other dangerous creatures lurking around corners were common. The place was swarming with them and sometimes turned answering nature's calls into small adventures in themselves.

From an early age, I had wanted to do something to alleviate the plight of those who had to go out into the open to relieve themselves. This probably played a small role in my choice of the sanitaryware sector when I was making the transition from trade to industry.

There were other more practical reasons. When we were considering various options, Dr G.P. Kane, senior advisor with the Directorate General of Technical Development of the Government of India, offered us three options—ceramic sanitaryware, insulators and refractories. Bhaiji and I selected ceramic sanitaryware as it was difficult to earn money in the other two. It was then a shot in the dark as we had no experience in or knowledge of any of the three industries. But almost six decades later, I can say that Bhaiji's speculative instinct, which had earned our family a lot of wealth and renown, was as sharp as ever. Today, my nephews and I together command more than half the market share for sanitaryware in the country.

India wasn't very industrialized at that time. The government, led by Pandit Jawaharlal Nehru, wanted public-sector-led development. Large, publicly funded projects and companies were called 'temples of modern India'. Pandit Nehru, who famously derided the profit motive, would often ask: 'Where is the money with the private sector?'

Young people today will find it difficult to comprehend the hostile business environment prevailing then. Socialism was the dogma of the time and its adherents were its high priests. Private industry was treated with suspicion and disdain but tolerated as a necessary evil. Consequently, there were few opportunities for ambitious young men to venture into industry.

As a result, India missed several waves of global growth and came to be labelled the 'sick man of Asia'. Imagine what we could have achieved if the thinking that propelled India to open up its economy in 1991 had dawned on the Indian political leadership in the early years of Independence. That was the time when our Southeast Asian neighbours embarked on a path of development and industrialization, which catapulted them into the ranks of the world's middle-income countries and lifted their people far above the levels we Indians could achieve. It was a wasted opportunity that set us back by decades. But all that is now water under the bridge.

An example will suffice. Shortly before we entered the sanitaryware industry, the Military Engineering Services Hospital in Chennai needed about forty pieces of sanitaryware urgently. Parry, with a factory close by, was the obvious supplier of choice. But it said it would take at least six months to supply the requirements. I don't blame Parry. Blinkered government policies that placed irrational caps on capacities were responsible. Till 1955, India was actually importing its entire sanitaryware requirements.

Dr Kane, an upright bureaucrat, was keen on encouraging Indian entrepreneurs to set up sanitaryware units to overcome the massive shortage in the country. After we had decided to enter the ceramics and sanitaryware industry, Dr Kane, who was in charge of giving us the necessary licence, told Bhaiji: 'You must tie up with a foreign collaborator for vitreous china, preferably with investment.'

Looking back after all these years, he was absolutely right.

We negotiated with American Standard, a global leader in the sector, to set up a sanitaryware unit in India as a 50:50 joint venture. The talks were going well and we were close to signing a definitive collaboration agreement. That's when American Standard's international business head, Raymond E. Walker, who was based in Paris, came up with a plan to have four different collaborations with four different Indian companies in the northern, southern, eastern and western regions of India. According to his proposal,

BRINGING THE RAINBOW

American Standard would hold a 50 per cent stake in each of the four companies. The balance 50 per cent was to be held by the regional collaborator as well as American Standard's partners from other regions.

We learnt that Mr Walker was negotiating collaborations with Bengal Potteries and some companies in southern India. Perhaps he wanted to hedge his bets by not putting all his eggs in one basket. Maybe he thought his plan would give his company a pan-Indian presence in the quickest possible time. We never learnt the logic behind his line of thinking, but Bhaiji and I thought the plan was a recipe for confusion and financial disaster. Not only would we not have a controlling interest in our company, the expected presence of representatives of rival companies on the board would severely constrain any future expansion plans. We told him flatly: 'Enough is enough. We don't want to collaborate with you.'

This meant we were back to square one. We had an in-principle approval from the government to set up a sanitaryware unit, but no foreign collaborator. Bhaiji then wrote to several people, including J.R.T. Hay, chairman of Twyfords Ltd, who had earlier worked in Calcutta for Hoare Miller, a managing agency. I remember he took several days to finalize the letter, which impressed Mr Hay, who wrote back saying he was willing to discuss the matter.

Fortunately, Onkar Bhaiji happened to be in London at that time. After a couple of meetings, Mr Hay decided to go with us. He had one simple condition: 'You must ensure that one family member moves to the location of the plant as supervision is essential for profits in the ceramics industry.'

His other piece of advice: 'Collaborate with a company that makes money in its native country.' Twyfords, which had a two-hundred-year-old heritage, was highly profitable.

We, too, had one condition. We wanted Twyfords to be a financial partner. That way, we reasoned, it would continue to take an interest in the long-term prospects of the venture.

Soon, a new company, Hindusthan Twyfords Ltd, was incorporated. The technical fee due to Twyfords was converted into equity, giving it a 26 per cent stake. The Somany family subscribed to 52 per cent, while the balance was with the public. The issue of ₹30 lakh was oversubscribed 78.1 times, a record in those days.

Official formalities and red tape were stifling in those days. Not only did the government decide what one could manufacture, it also decided the capacity of the unit as well as its location. We secured permission to set up our factory in Durgapur, an industrial hub near Calcutta. Because of our foreign collaboration, there was also an export obligation.

However, most of the raw material for our unit would be coming from Rajasthan and Gujarat. Moreover, Delhi was a big distribution centre for sanitaryware. Meanwhile, Hindusthan National Glass had got permission to set up its unit in Ghaziabad. So we began to look for land in Punjab (Haryana had still not been carved out of this state) and Uttar Pradesh and finally settled on a 95-acre plot of land in Bahadurgarh in what is now Haryana. The land was fallow, so it wasn't being used for agriculture. There was a village on one side and nullah on the other. Most importantly, there was a railway siding nearby.

When we had acquired about 40 per cent of the land, rumours began to swirl that the Birlas were setting up the plant. People refused to sell us land unless we paid a much higher price than what we were offering. This would have raised costs and made the project unviable. We approached Partap Singh Kairon, the then chief minister of Punjab; B.M. Birla wrote a letter introducing us to him. After hearing us out, he agreed that the project was good for the state as it would spur industrialization and create employment. He gave Mohanlal Sodhani, our liaison man, a special pass to move around the secretariat to push the file from desk to desk.

Kairon was not only chief minister, but also the tallest leader of Punjab. He was also honest to the core. Not once did he or anyone of consequence demand a single rupee from us. Politicians and bureaucrats, steeped in nationalism and fired by the ideals of nation building, gladly went out of their way to expedite matters they thought were in the national interest.

The only help we provided was to supply Kairon with karela (bitter gourd) from Calcutta to keep his diabetes in check. Those were the days before the Green Revolution and procuring good-quality karela in Punjab wasn't easy.

Sodhani did, however, have to spend small amounts of money to pay off the peons who carried the files and some lower-level clerks who processed them. They wouldn't even deliver our visiting cards to the concerned officials or open the files on our project without this speed money.

The situation is very different in government offices across the country now. The cancer of corruption spread rapidly during the Emergency. Bribes, which were rare in the years prior to that, became the norm and the rates increased suddenly as businessmen were told that the 'risks had increased'.

In Delhi, we had to procure an import licence for the machinery we wanted to import. Our file had to be placed before the licensing committee. Then, the public issue needed clearances from the Controller of Capital Issues. And the plans needed the approval of the Directorate General of Technical Development. There were layers upon layers of bureaucracy that our proposal had to be steered through.

Sodhani went about his task manfully and managed to get all clearances and licences, but the process delayed our plans slightly. Again, we didn't have to pay any significant amount of speed money, except for some loose change to peons and lower-level clerks, to get the approvals.

Bhaiji and I were clear that we wanted only the best and the latest technology as we didn't want to compromise on the quality of our products. ICICI, then India's premier development financial institution, extended a ₹27-lakh foreign exchange loan, which we used to pay for imported kilns, sieving equipment, glaze mixers, blungers (raw-material mixers) and some specialized magnets to extract iron particles.

Bhaiji had commenced work on building the factory while I was still in England. Upon my return, the responsibility of carrying this work forward fell on my young shoulders. I had never been to Delhi before, except on my visits to Chirawa. But there was no question of saying no to my eldest brother. Since the family had reposed its confidence in me, I had to deliver. If that meant having to move bag, baggage and wife to Delhi, it had to be done. So, soon after returning from England, I moved to Delhi, which is now my permanent home. However, I retain close links with the city I was born and bred in. Hindusthan Twyfords (now HSIL) and all my privately held investment companies are registered in Calcutta, which also remains my tax base.

I plunged headlong into the task of building the factory within days of moving to Delhi. Bhaiji had already commenced construction and a warehouse had been partially built. I had just completed almost six months of training in England, learning the intricacies of the ceramics industry. Now, I had to teach myself the nitty-gritty of civil construction. Every day, I would encounter dozens of technical terms that were completely Greek to me. So I bought a technical dictionary, which I carried with me constantly over the next several months. I must have consulted it thousands of times, so much so that I soon became something of an expert on construction-industry jargon. I also had to teach myself to read and understand technical drawings.

Learning the technicalities of civil construction was one thing. Getting timely work out of civil contractors was quite another. I found, much to my dismay and disgust, that most contractors had no sense of time. They would promise to arrive at the factory at 8 a.m. This meant I had to leave my flat in Delhi between 6 a.m. and 6.30 a.m., which, in turn, meant waking up even earlier. Fortunately, I have always been an early riser. But imagine my consternation—and that of my colleagues, including a few Englishmen who had come from Twyfords to help us set up and run the factory—when the contractor would finally land up at 5.30 p.m., almost tens hours late.

'*Sa'ab, galti ho gaya,*' was all they would say.

They didn't look particularly sorry. I found this habit very annoying, being a stickler myself for punctuality, but had to grin and bear it.

In Calcutta, where I had interacted commercially with peers and with white-collar workers, it was the practice, especially among Marwaris, to conduct business on the basis of mutual trust. Transactions worth lakhs of rupees would be carried out on the strength of this trust. Word-of-mouth commitments were sacrosanct and rarely, if ever, broken. I understand that this practice is still the norm among some sections of the business community in Calcutta.

But in Delhi, even the smallest detail had to be put down on paper and signed. This was new to me, and along with the chronic lack of punctuality, a huge culture shock. But I laboured on, determined not to let circumstances get the better of me. It was difficult going, but I didn't give up.

The civil construction fell a few months behind schedule. On quizzing the contractor, I came to learn that the civil architect we had engaged, Kothari Associates, had not delivered the plans as promised. On digging a little deeper, I discovered the root cause of the delay. Making a template design and replicating it across several locations was an easy, swift and cost-effective option for architects. Since the foundation required for each individual piece of heavy machinery in our plant had to be drawn and designed separately, the firm was taking its time.

This was unacceptable. The delay was costing us money and every day's delay in construction meant an equivalent delay in hitting the market with our products. I went to meet Mr N.K. Kothari, the senior partner of the firm. He refused to discuss the matter with me. I am normally a very calm person and rarely lose my cool, but I could feel my temper rising. Making a special effort to control myself, I requested him to introduce me to the architects who were drawing up the plans for me. He refused again. I left his office in a huff. The next day I received a telegram from Kothari Associates informing me that 'we are no longer your architects'.

By this time, I had built a good personal equation with the contractor who was building our plant. In the course of a conversation and, perhaps, without really meaning to, he gave me a stunning piece of information. 'I have a special arrangement with Kothari under which I am supposed to pay him 1.5 per cent of the contract value,' he told me one day. I was speechless. Then, as now, Kothari Associates was a large and reputed firm of architects. To have such an 'arrangement' with a civil contractor was irregular, to say the least.

Meanwhile, work at the plant had almost ground to a halt on account of the drawings that never arrived. If I could get hold of the contract between Kothari and the contractor, I figured, I could force him back to work and thus salvage something from this increasingly murky and sordid state of affairs.

I befriended a junior executive in the architect's office and through him, managed to get a copy of the contract. I was ready to confront Mr Kothari.

But when I did, he refused to budge from his stand of not completing the project. I could have dragged him to court. The copy of the contract I had procured would have made my case even stronger. But it would have meant more delays and my first priority was to get my factory up and running. I left his office after an almighty row.

Fortunately, I found another architect who completed the drawings I needed in double quick time. The factory was finally ready to begin production, but the delays had cost us a precious three to four months.

We were new players in the industry, our brand, H Vitreous, was unknown and we had only a handful of dealers across India. On the face of it, the odds seemed stacked against us. But there were some factors working in our favour as well. There was a massive shortage of sanitaryware in the market as the government had banned imports a few years previously to save precious foreign exchange. The few existing domestic players, such as Parry, Parshuram and Khodiyar were making earthen sanitaryware. Our vitreous products were far superior in looks, finish, durability and overall quality than the earthen sanitaryware of our competitors, and therefore, a much better value proposition in spite of the higher price.

We launched around twenty-five new products in the market. They stood out among all competing products, generated good demand and allowed us to quickly establish a name for ourselves.

Initially, our production was low. We began with only sixty pieces a day, but quickly scaled up to three hundred units daily and then to a thousand units. Since our products were far superior to the competition we were able to capture market share, riding on the 'demand pull' for our products.

As we rapidly ramped up production, Hindusthan Twyfords began to benefit from the economies of scale. We cut prices, passing the benefits of scale to the consumers, while being able to maintain our strong margins. Prices of H Vitreous basins, commodes and Indian pans came down by an average of 57 per cent over a period of eighteen to twenty months. Shorn of jargon, this meant we were selling our products at less than half the retail price we had started out with.

Demand soared. We had to grapple with a huge backlog of orders, and despite my best efforts, production couldn't keep pace with demand.

Older readers will recall that Socialist India was characterized by shortages of almost everything. This led to a burgeoning black market for every conceivable product. 'Blackmarketeer' was a common term of abuse. Bollywood aficionados will remember that heroes from the black-and-white era were strident crusaders against this menace.

Given the combination of rising demand for Hindusthan Twyfords products and our inability to satisfy it fully, it was perhaps natural that some dealers began charging a premium on

BRINGING THE RAINBOW

our products. When I learnt about this, I summarily terminated their dealerships and appointed new ones. Many people told me I was being foolish. 'If people are willing to pay more for your products, why are you saying no?' I was asked incredulously.

I strongly disagreed with them. By introducing vitreous china in the Indian market, Hindusthan Twyfords had given Indian consumers a product that was at par with the best available in the developed western world. Then, by passing on the benefits of falling production costs to consumers, we had created a value proposition that was, if not unique, very rare in the early 1960s—world-class products at prices Indian consumers considered affordable. The rising demand and the order backlog proved that we were riding a crest. Allowing rampant black-marketing would give us higher short-term profits, albeit illegally, but would seriously, and negatively, affect the bonds we were beginning to establish with our customers. It would also hand over, or at the minimum, substantially cede, pricing power to middlemen, who, I was under no illusions, would squeeze us relentlessly.

There was another reason as well. I was inordinately proud of the Somany family's good reputation in Calcutta. Bhaiji had obtained his membership at the Calcutta Stock Exchange solely on the strength of my father's good reputation and standing. This kind of goodwill takes decades to build, but can be destroyed in minutes.

I was new to Delhi. No one knew me or my family in the city. So it was up to me to establish for myself and my family the same reputation and goodwill that my predecessors had acquired in Calcutta. Once again, I was faced with a matter of principle. I went with my gut instinct, which, I'm glad to say in retrospect, proved to be beneficial over the long term.

I am grateful to God that early in my career, because of this experience, I learnt the true worth of long-term value creation over the attraction of short-term profits. This incident also led me to introduce another 'innovation', which has now become a standard practice across many sectors—the setting of a maximum retail price (MRP).

Far from losing our shirts, as many naysayers had predicted when we chose to launch vitreous ceramic sanitaryware, we were gaining market share and setting the terms of trade in an industry in which we were still newcomers. It was this stupendous consumer support that gave me the confidence to set the terms for extending cash discounts, which I have described in a previous chapter.

Perhaps driven by our rising profile and market share, our competitors, all of whom produced earthenware, also tied up with foreign collaborators to launch their own vitreous china products. Parry tied up with UK-based Doulton, which had had a large import-led presence in India prior to Independence, while Parshuram and Khodiyar, which were owned by the same family, got their technology from France's Porcher. Another company, Neyvelli Ceramics, promoted by Seshasayee Paper & Boards, also entered the ceramics and sanitaryware industry in collaboration with Keranag of West Germany.

The competition was hotting up. I realized that we needed to offer something more in order to retain the lead we had established with our superior technology. In those days, sanitaryware design was very basic and functional. As we gained market share and confidence, Hindusthan Twyfords began to introduce new product designs. We were the first in India to launch an anti-splash rim for washbasins, concealed wall hangers for washbasins and urinals and semi-pierced tap holes in washbasins. These design innovations provided a lot more value to consumers without burdening us with too much additional cost. For example, basins were then simply screwed on to walls. Over time, the exposed screws would rust and the putty around them would chip off. This would make for very ugly viewing. Our new design added a touch of class to our products and lent a new elegance to bathrooms.

Soon after we launched our new products, one R.M. Mehra of Neyvelli Ceramics wrote to Bhaiji, who was the chairman of Hindusthan Twyfords and based in Calcutta, charging us with infringing his patents on semi-pierced tap holes and concealed hangers. Bhaiji passed the missive on to me. I was appalled. We had obtained the designs from Twyfords, which had been selling these products in its home and export markets for years. A few other western brands also had similar products. How could Neyvelli Ceramics claim a patent over common knowledge?

I was determined to overturn its patent claim in a court of law, if necessary. After discussing the matter internally, I even considered hiring and bringing in a patent lawyer from England to represent us. Finally, however, I selected senior lawyer N.K. Anand, of the law firm Anand & Anand to fight for Hindusthan Twyfords.

Imagine my surprise when Mr Anand reported back that the patent numbers Mr Mehra had quoted were wrong. I filed a suit against Neyvelli Ceramics in the Delhi High Court, which set up a commission of enquiry to investigate the matter.

I found a Czech brochure from 1955 showing semi-pierced tap holes. I submitted this and 108 kg of brochures from Twyfords and other foreign manufacturers in support of my claim that these designs had been around for years and that Neyvelli Ceramics could not claim a patent over them. Mr Mehra countered by suing Hindusthan Twyfords in the Madras High Court.

While the matter was still being adjudicated upon by the two high courts, I met Mr Mehra for the first time at a meeting of the Rotary Club in Calcutta, which I had joined a few years earlier. After exchanging pleasantries, Mr Mehra took me aside and said: '*Aap to bade ziddi ho. Sunte nahi ho. Bhai se mila do.*' ('You are very stubborn and so don't listen. Take me to your brother.')

His proposal, at the meeting, was outrageously bold but completely unacceptable to me.

'Let me charge one rupee per annum as licence fee from every company, except Hindusthan Twyfords, for the use of my patents,' he told Bhaiji.

I was adamant. 'I'll accept this proposal over my dead body,' I told Bhaiji in Mr Mehra's presence. My '*zid*' (stubbornness) was on a principle and I wasn't going to compromise on it.

I was proved right. The Delhi and Madras high courts both ruled in favour of Hindusthan Twyfords. Mr Mehra did not pursue his legal fight in the higher courts. So the matter ended there.

But our sparring continued. He was the convenor of a sanitaryware sub-committee in the civil-engineering division of the Indian Standards Institution, subsequently renamed the Bureau of Indian Standards. I was a member of this sub-committee, and found his views on several issues completely out of tune with the times.

Once, after yet another heated argument at a meeting of the sub-committee, I told him in front of all the members: 'Mr Chairman, you are outdated.'

This became a regular feature of our interactions, but our 'fights' were over principles. Mr Mehra finally retired and moved to Bombay, but we kept in touch. He was a well-read man and had, over his lifetime, collected hundreds of priceless technical books and journals on the sanitaryware industry. Later, he sold me his entire collection for about ₹10,000. I still have the collection in the library of my plant in Somanypuram, Bibinagar, in Telangana.

Meanwhile, Hindusthan Twyfords had gone from strength to strength. In 1964–65, we were in a position to prepay the loans we had taken from banks and other financial institutions. It was the first time I signed a cheque for a crore of rupees. Even today, a crore is not a sum to be sneezed at. Fifty years ago, it was an unimaginably large amount. I remember savouring the elation I felt while signing the cheque.

A year later, I faced the first major crisis in my fledgling career as an industrialist. Our collaboration with Twyfords had ended the previous year and the company had been renamed Hindustan Sanitaryware and Industries Ltd (HSIL). A kiln had broken down with a full load of sanitaryware products inside. The temperature inside the kiln was more than 1,200°C. Our team of engineers had no idea how to repair the kiln and, in any case, it was impossible to enter the chamber till it had cooled.

We were losing production and lots of money each day the plant remained idle. On the eleventh day, I decided to take matters into my own hands. The temperature inside the kiln was still 120°C, but I decided to enter it. My colleagues warned me against it. I told them: 'Since no one is willing to enter, and I can't order anyone to do so, I will have to do it myself.' I had, meanwhile, studied the literature that had come with the kiln when we had imported it a few years earlier and figured out what needed to be done.

It was a harrowing experience. My hair started singeing as soon as I entered the chamber, but I somehow managed to carry out the necessary repairs and got the plant back on its feet. HSIL lost a month of production, but quickly bounced back.

I have been extremely lucky with my career at HSIL. When I entered the industry, I didn't have to face much competition. This allowed me to quickly establish my brand. Then, I didn't have to face any of the major industrial or other problems that have plagued many other companies. I also didn't face any serious failures as we entered the market with a good product and a technology that was years ahead of what my competitors offered. A combination of these very fortuitous factors allowed me to succeed in a new industry.

7

MY PERSONAL LIFE

It is the custom in most Marwari families to marry early. Soon after I passed I. Com in 1956, my grandmother, the matriarch of the Somany clan, suffered a paralytic stroke. So everyone wanted me to get married and settle down. I was then about nineteen years old, but was clear in my mind that I would marry only after completing my education and joining the family business.

In early 1959, about six months after graduating with a bachelor of commerce degree, the family elders negotiated my marriage with Krishna Mohta, whose family was well regarded in Calcutta's Marwari circles. On a crisp winter morning, I made my way to the Mohta residence on Elgin Road, a posh address in south Calcutta, where my prospective wife lived in a joint family comprising her parents and several uncles, aunts, siblings and cousins. I was accompanied by Bhaiji, his wife Kamla Bhabi and two other family elders.

This was to be our first meeting. At her house, I was asked to wait in a room by myself while the elders were led to another room to meet the Mohta clan. The plan was for the two of us to meet without having to endure the embarrassment of curious relatives gawking at us, providing 'helpful' cues for conversation and making merry at our obvious discomfiture.

After about half an hour, Kamla Bhabi signalled it was time to leave. On our way home, she asked: 'How was the girl?'

'Which girl?' I asked.

Krishna, it seems, had a last minute attack of 'stage fright' and didn't come out to meet me.

Bhabi and the others were shocked. 'Why didn't you tell us?' they demanded.

'It was your arrangement. What can I do?' I responded.

This little comedy of errors had a happy ending a few days later, when another meeting was set up. I went back to the Mohta residence, this time accompanied only by Kamla Bhabi, and met Krishna.

I had two conditions: she wasn't fluent in English, so she would have to take spoken English classes; and she had to finish her schooling. I knew I would be leaving for England shortly and after completing my training there, would have to work in Delhi. So it was important that she should not only speak, read and understand English, but also have the basic education necessary for her to be able to conduct herself in a cosmopolitan society.

I married Krishna on 16 February 1959. Unlike now, when many Marwari (and other) families use these occasions to show off their wealth and connections, marriages then were simple ceremonies. My *baraat* was about forty- or fifty-people strong and comprised family members and some school friends.

Honeymoons weren't very popular then and we didn't go on one. Instead, we visited Darjeeling that May—our first holiday together—and stayed at Windamere, a charming hotel that did not take in Indian guests till Independence.

The dynamics of Indian joint families are usually decided by the women of the family and our family was no different. We brothers would leave for work every morning and return late every evening. The women would stay at home and their interpersonal equations determined whether families stayed together or broke up into smaller nuclear units.

My grandmother, a strong personality and the unquestioned matriarch of the family, passed away in 1959. She was very strict, but always gave all of us lots of love. My mother had never interfered with her daughters-in-law, and had allowed Kamla Bhabi to run the house. All the other wives got along well with each other and accepted Kamla Bhabi as the first among equals.

Krishna settled quickly into the Somany household. We would often go out for movies and eat out on weekends. Sometimes, we would be accompanied by other members of the family, but often, it would be just the two of us. Since we hadn't gone through a period of courtship prior to our marriage, this helped us bond and get to know one another.

It was an almost idyllic existence and lasted a little more than a year. In 1961, we moved to England, and upon our return about six months later, to Delhi.

Life in the National Capital was a huge change from what we were used to in Calcutta. Both of us came from joint families. Our houses were always teeming with people—brothers, sisters, their spouses and children, and guests. I had a close group of friends with whom I would spend some of my weekends. Krishna, too, had a few friends she would socialize with.

Both of us came from established business families, so we had always had a large retinue of domestic helps to assist with daily chores.

In Delhi, we didn't have even a distant relative or acquaintance. I rented a four-bedroom flat on the first floor of a house in Uttari Marg near Gangaram Hospital. I also rented two barsatis (a single room plus bath and a mini kitchen) in the same house—and used one as a home office and the other as a room for the domestic help.

I would usually leave home every morning at 8 a.m. and return twelve hours later—sometimes even later than that. But I would also work from home once or twice a week, meeting architects, going through drawings, corresponding with suppliers and sending reports to my brothers. I would thus get to spend a few hours more with Krishna.

It was a very difficult period for her. She often felt very lonely as time hung heavy on her hands. Unlike in England, where we had spent six months, Delhi did not have 24x7 television. National broadcaster Doordarshan had begun experimental telecasts on 15 September 1959, but regular daily broadcasts would begin only six years later.

This could have led to a permanent schism in our relationship. But I was fortunate that during the six months we spent in England—both of us felt it was a belated but extended honeymoon—my wife also became my best friend. Propinquity obviously played a large role in this development. But fate has been kind to me on several counts. This was one of them. Of course, I didn't know then that the stars that had showered so much good fortune on me early in my life would also deal a body blow to me a decade-and-a-half later.

As I have written earlier, we didn't know anyone in Delhi. The atmosphere in Calcutta was very informal. Delhi was very different. I asked around, found out about a ladies' club nearby and introduced Krishna to it. Soon she built up a close circle of acquaintances who she would meet twice a month.

Krishna was an excellent cook and was good at dishing out all kinds of cuisine. Her ladies' club would organize a mela every year where members would put up stalls selling food and other items. The melas would be held on the lawns of Chemsford Club, Ashoka Hotel and a few other places. On every single occasion, Krishna's stall would be the first to sell its entire stock of food.

Meanwhile, I was getting very bogged down with work and realized that I, too, needed to get a life. So, I joined the Junior Chamber movement in 1963. The Junior Chamber, more popularly known as Jaycees, is a not-for-profit foundation that was established in the United States in 1920 to teach young people in the 18–40 age group, leadership, management, community service and self-development.

I learnt a lot and made many new friends in the years I spent at the Delhi chapter of Jaycees. It was there that I learnt how to draft agenda papers, write minutes of meetings and conduct public meetings, including annual general meetings. It was a fantastic training ground and enabled me to learn these critical skills, which, unfortunately, our educational and professional institutes do not teach. These proved invaluable to me later, when I became, first a director and later, chairman of HSIL. These lessons also helped me immensely in carrying out my duties as president of the Punjab & Haryana Chambers of Commerce and Industry as well as a member of the various public committees in which I have served over the last five decades.

I was elected president of the Delhi chapter of Jaycees after four years, having previously served as treasurer, secretary and vice president. During my term as president, I suggested organizing public-speaking courses for members.

We would hold our meetings every weekend at YMCA. I remember being asked once to speak extempore on peacocks. The next speaker could very well be asked to speak on nuclear disarmament and the third on the then ongoing debate on whether or not to ban big-game hunting. The topics were chosen at random. There was no Internet in those days to help one conduct quick research on a topic. So, everyone had to come prepared on a wide variety of subjects, inevitably leading to an improvement in the reading habits of members.

There were several occasions when participants, myself included, faltered in our speeches and failed to make an impact. But no one laughed or sniggered. It could be their turn next.

The upshot of this was that we lost our inhibitions and as we gained confidence, we all became better public speakers. These lessons learnt all those decades ago have helped me immensely throughout my life. I had reason to thank Jaycees again recently, when I was asked to address, without any preparation, students at Chitkara University, Punjab, on attrition. I could do so, in front of close to a thousand students, only because of the training I had received in the mid-1960s and the constant honing of this skill over the years.

During my presidency of the Delhi chapter of Jaycees in 1967, I undertook a long thirty-five-day tour of Europe and the US scouting for technology and machinery for HSIL. I was in Cleveland, Ohio, in the States when I received an invitation from the local chapter of Jaycees to address a meeting as a guest. I politely declined the offer as I had a flight to catch. The president of the local chapter wouldn't take no for an answer. 'Mr Somany, don't worry. We will reschedule your flight and ensure that you don't miss your next appointment,' he said.

That evening, he sent a car to ferry me to the meeting. About seventy members were present. India had just devalued the rupee. They wanted to know more about it. I spoke for about half an hour and also fielded some questions from the members present. This was my first exposure to public speaking outside India and I remember feeling proud at having given a good account of myself before a foreign audience.

After the meeting, the members arranged for me to be dropped to the airport, where I took a later flight, which they had arranged, to my next destination.

I remember another occasion, this time in June 2005. I had gone to Geneva to address a conference of the International Labour Organization (ILO) as a representative of Indian employers. About 179 countries were present at the conference and each speaker was given eight minutes to have their say. The timekeeper cut off the mike at the end of the allotted time.

My speech, which I had taken a few days to write and which I had rehearsed several times, was over the time limit by fifteen seconds. Despite trying hard, I couldn't compress it any further. A gentleman, Mr I.P. Anand, who was a senior executive of the Thapar Group, knew the chairperson of the conference well.

Mr Anand introduced me to her and said: 'Madam, Mr Somany has a problem...' She graciously allowed me the extra time.

Who said connections don't work in the West?

Meanwhile, in 1963, we moved from our rented flat in Uttari Marg to a rented house in Defence Colony, which was a little more spacious. By this time, I had a fairly large circle of friends and acquaintances. The business was doing well and friends told me I should think of buying a house. But I had neither the money nor the time to do so.

My daily routine continued to remain packed with meetings, appointments and other engagements. I had taken on several new responsibilities at public organizations, such as Jaycees, the Rotary Club and chambers of commerce, for which I had to find time.

Consequently, I still couldn't devote sufficient time to my wife and home. So I decided that come what may, I wouldn't work on Sundays and that I would reserve the day solely for my family. This might seem odd today, when so much is being written about maintaining a work-life balance, but when you are establishing a business from scratch in a new city, you have to give it all you have, work day and night and make huge personal sacrifices to give yourself some chance of success. That's what I did. I was fortunate in having a wife who understood my circumstances and stood by my side.

Delhi was still a new city for us. It wasn't the bustling metro it is today and Defence Colony, then on the outskirts of the city, was a sleepy, tree-lined neighbourhood, with only a few single and two-storeyed houses owned mainly by retired defence personnel. It also did not have any of the tony restaurants that have now come to characterize it. Nonetheless, on Sundays, Krishna and I would set out in my Ambassador and go shopping, catch a movie and eat out before returning home in the evenings.

Sandip, my son, was born on 16 December 1963 at Sharma Nursing Home in Calcutta, not far from our residence on Gurusaday Road. We had decided to have our first baby in Calcutta as our families were still based there and Krishna would have family members around to attend to any medical or other issues that may have developed.

Unfortunately, I couldn't be there to witness the arrival of my first-born. Hindusthan Twyfords was holding its first sales conference at the Imperial Hotel in Delhi on 16 and 17 December that year and had invited 150 dealers from across India. The conference had been fixed months in advance, so there was no question of cancelling or postponing it.

I arrived in Calcutta on the night of 17 December and saw my son for the first time two days after he was born. 'Another addition to the family; another manager is born,' Bhaiji said with his usual practical logic.

I returned to Delhi with Krishna and Sandip three days later.

I wrote to the principal of St Columba's School, a leading boys' school in Delhi, the day Sandip was born. A few days later, I received a reply saying the school did not have any system of booking a seat in advance and that I should apply for admission when my son came of age.

Sandip's birth meant I had to change my daily routine, so that I would be able to spend more time at home with my family. I began to return home at 5 p.m. Krishna and I would go out for walks every evening with Sandip in a pram. When he was a little older, we did the usual things that parents do, like taking him to the zoo or the rail museum.

We had, by this time, moved to a lovely two-storeyed rented house in Greater Kailash I. Our next-door neighbours had several children with whom Sandip would play.

When the time came to enrol him in school, I discovered that it wasn't an easy task. Though the competition wasn't as stiff as it is now, it was still quite strong. However, St Columba's, which was our choice of school, gave preference to relatives of students already studying there.

The Kejriwal family of Calcutta had been our family friends for many years. They, too, hailed from Chirawa. Ram Kumar Kejriwal, the patriarch of the family, served as a director on the board of Hindusthan National Glass. His grandson was studying in St Columba's. I contacted Ram Kumar Kejriwal's son, Chandra Kishore, who told me to speak to his wife Bimla.

'Let me find out more about the admission procedure,' she said.

After some time, she told me: 'The only option is to show you as a relative and show my address as yours.'

Sandip did well in his entrance examination, but Bimla Kejriwal's help made it easier than it otherwise might have been. I changed his address three years after he was admitted.

Sandhya was born four years after Sandip, on 6 June 1967, at Woodlands Multispeciality Hospital in Calcutta. In a strange twist of fate, I couldn't be present to welcome the arrival of my second-born too. Some urgent work cropped up in Delhi and I had to leave Calcutta on 5 June. I returned to Calcutta two days later and brought Krishna, Sandip and Sandhya back to Delhi.

I had a full house in Delhi now. Krishna had her hands full bringing up two young children, looking after the household and also continuing her involvement with the ladies' club, where she had made several good friends who had become part of our regular social circle.

A year after Sandhya was born, in 1968, we went on a family vacation to Manali and stayed at a recently set up tourist cottage, which cost us ₹175 per night. When I see the rate cards of the various hotels I stay in, I realize how much inflation has eaten into the innards of our economy. But, like death and taxes, inflation is one fact of life that everyone has to face and deal with.

While on vacation, I learnt that Svetoslav Nikolaevich Roerich, the celebrated Russian painter who had made India his home, and his filmstar wife Devika Rani, arguably the most popular actress of the 1930s and 1940s, were visiting their charming hill estate on the outskirts of Manali.

I had, for long, greatly admired both their work. On an impulse, Krishna and I drove over to meet them. It was a long shot. Devika Rani had become a recluse since her marriage to Roerich in 1945 and the closure of Bombay Talkies, the iconic Bollywood studio she and her first husband, film-maker Himanshu Rai, had set up in 1934.

There was no guarantee that we would get an audience with the world famous couple who doggedly avoided the limelight and jealously guarded their privacy.

To our utter delight and considerable surprise, they not only agreed to meet us but also invited us inside their mansion for tea. They made a wonderful couple, full of warmth and radiating intelligence. Both of them were very well informed about diverse subjects and the conversation flowed. After about an hour, we bid them adieu. I never got to meet them again, but the afternoon we spent with them remains etched in my memory almost half a century later.

My youngest daughter, Divya, was born on 5 November 1971 in Delhi at Sharma Nursing Home in Greater Kailash.

Soon, the children were all enrolled in school. Sandip studied in St Columba's, and my daughters in Convent of Jesus and Mary, a well-known missionary school for girls in Delhi. Sandip was an average student, but fortunately, like me, he developed a reading habit early. Both my daughters, however, were good at studies.

Krishna and I took a keen interest in their progress. I would help them with mathematics, English and geography while Krishna would tutor them in Hindi and Sanskrit.

The children had settled into a routine. They made friends at school and had a happy existence. Meanwhile, the family continued to prosper. We brothers were considered closely bonded, despite one or two fault lines that would cause much trouble later, and jointly owned all our businesses. But over the last decade, Surendra Kumar had moved to Bombay, Lalit to Ahmedabad and I was based in Delhi. Bhaiji, Onkar Bhaiji and Chandra Kumar had stayed on in Calcutta. As the family had dispersed, our children were growing up without much interaction with the rest of the family and without getting to know their cousins. Bhaiji didn't like this and made it a point to invite all of us brothers and our families to spend a few weeks every summer with him in Calcutta. Krishna would take the children and spend two or three weeks there. I would join them for a few days as my business and other commitments did not allow for long absences from Delhi.

In 1974, Krishna and the children had gone to Calcutta for their annual summer tryst with the rest of the family. I was scheduled to join them a few days later. On 1 July, I was in a meeting at my factory in Bahadurgarh when I received a call from my nephew's wife. 'Mamiji is not well. Please proceed to Calcutta immediately.'

Bhaiji was in Kenya, so there was no one I could turn to. With misgivings in my heart, I took the earliest available flight to Calcutta. But I was too late.

Krishna had passed away.

When the shock passed, I tried to find out what had happened. She had been in perfect health when she had left Delhi. She seemed to have been in no discomfort even moments before her death.

Krishna, I was told, was getting ready for a bath. They found her on the bathroom floor. Her nails and lips had turned blue.

Had she been poisoned? Had she consumed it herself or was it administered to her by someone else? How would I bring up three young children all by myself? These disturbing thoughts were gnawing away at me.

I stayed back in Calcutta for ten days and then returned to Delhi with my three children after the period of mourning and after completing the necessary rituals.

Kamla Bhabi and my mother accompanied us to Delhi. Bhabi returned to Calcutta after three weeks, but Mother stayed on for a few more days.

It was a very difficult phase in my life. Fate had showered me with good fortune all my life and had given me much more than I probably deserved. It had given me plenty of professional success, all the worldly comforts I could hope for, a very warm and loving wife who had become my best friend and three bright young children.

Running a growing business, carrying out the public responsibilities I had taken up and bringing up three children, including two young daughters, was an extremely difficult task. The prospect of my children growing up in the care of hired help wasn't an appealing one.

I tried for a few months to return home from work by 3 p.m. to be with my children when they returned home from school. I would bring work home but found after a few days that this wasn't a viable long-term solution as I was failing to do justice to both my children and my work.

A cruel blow had suddenly shattered my happy and well-ordered life. I was feeling the strain and it must have begun to show in my behaviour.

Kamla Bhabi asked me one day: 'What do you wish to do?'

I knew at once what she meant and replied: 'I don't want to remarry.'

But the family mounted pressure on me to remarry, if not for myself then at least for the sake of my children. After resisting for a while, I finally agreed after a long talk with Bhaiji.

But it was easier said than done. India was still very conservative in the mid-1970s. Most families were reluctant to consider a widower with three children as a match for their daughter.

Finally, my family selected a girl called Lata from Pune. Surendra Kumar, my Bombay-based brother, his wife and I went to meet her. She was college-educated and working at a Kirloskar Group company and came from a well-regarded family.

I married Lata on 19 June, 1975 and soon after, we flew to Calcutta. I felt uneasy going back, to the same house where Krishna had died, as I still didn't know the real cause of her death.

My brothers organized a small reception in Calcutta on 20 June, to which we invited only our family and some close friends.

Over the next couple of days, Bhaiji suggested we transfer a certain sum of money into Lata's account so that she wouldn't have to turn to me for her needs.

On 24 June, I was in the office completing the transfer formalities when I received a call from home saying Lata wasn't feeling well. She was dead by the time my brothers and I returned home.

Like Krishna, her nails had turned blue.

This was the second death, under very mysterious circumstances, within a year. It was the same house. The same set of people and Kamla Bhabi were present at the time of death.

I was numb with shock. So were the children. What had

happened? My mind was in a whirl with all kinds of disturbing thoughts. It was almost as if fate was mocking me for the good fortune I had enjoyed till the previous year.

A few months later, some members of my family broached the topic of remarriage once again. They also mounted pressure on me to marry the widow of my youngest brother Lalit, who had died in 1972.

I flatly refused. We don't have a culture among Marwaris of marrying a sibling's widow and I didn't want to take any step that could lead to a messy situation in the future. But the problems that had forced me to agree to marry Lata came back to haunt me—a rapidly expanding business and growing children, especially two young girls. How was I to manage?

My health began to suffer as I tried to balance the conflicting needs of my profession and my children.

Kamla Bhabi said: 'You don't look good. Your health is breaking down.' Again, she wanted me to remarry.

My son was a teenager by then. My daughters were also growing up. Any decision I took would need a buy-in from them as well. Kamla Bhabi spoke to my daughters, who said they would have no problem if I married again. Sandip, too, said he would not have any objection to me remarrying. But I sensed an unspoken hesitation in his response.

Bhaiji, whose views I have always considered with respect, also joined the debate and said I should remarry. 'Otherwise, your children will suffer. They have their education and their lives ahead of them.' Then, there was the question of my two daughters. Beyond a point, they wouldn't be able to discuss their issues with me. They would need a mother to guide them.

The family selected a girl from Delhi. Snehlata was highly

educated. She held a Master's degree in Sanskrit and had also done her B. Ed. This would make her the most educated member of our family.

I married her on 21 February 1977.

I am grateful to Snehlata for selflessly stepping into Krishna's shoes and being the perfect mother to my three children. Divya, who was about three years old when Krishna passed away, has no recollections of her biological mother. My third wife, she says emphatically, was the only mother she knew and bonded closely with.

Sandip and Sandhya were older, being fourteen and ten years old when I married Snehlata, who gave them ample love and affection. Sandhya, too, like Divya, has no hesitation in saying that Snehlata gave her all the love and affection as well as guidance that a biological mother would have.

'I was old enough to realize that she was my stepmother. In fact, I clearly remembered—and still do—my own mother. But I must say, in all fairness, that not once did she give me any reason to miss my biological mother. For this, I'm thankful to god and to her,' Sandhya told me once.

Though relations between Sandip and Snehlata were cordial and natural, I sometimes thought I detected the slightest bit of hesitation on Sandip's part in acknowledging her. It is never easy to accept anyone as a replacement for a natural parent and he must have gone through moments of angst. I can only conjecture about this because we never actually discussed it. Fortunately, this never boiled over and he continued to give her the respect due to a mother till the very end.

A few years later, in 1983, I bought my first house, in Delhi's Safdarjung Enclave, after living in rented houses for almost a quarter of a century.

Whenever my friends would ask me why I wasn't buying a house, I would say: 'Fools build houses; wise men live in them.'

I wasn't just being facetious. As I have mentioned earlier, I had insisted on completing my graduation as I wanted to have the option of being able to take up a job in case my businesses failed. I had also refused to marry before graduation as I had wanted to be in a position to support my wife and family in case I needed to take up employment in a company in which I had no ownership stake.

I could have bought a house with HSIL funds, but had resisted the temptation. I wanted to buy my house with my own money. Why?

When coal mines were nationalized in the 1970s, there were instances of former mine-owners being stopped on the road and being asked to get out of cars owned by their companies, as these had become government property. I didn't want to face a situation where I would lose my home if I lost control of my company. Meanwhile, I had invested my money in other instruments that had given me handsome returns over a quarter of a century.

I wanted a 1,000-square-yard plot but couldn't afford it; so, I settled for a 500 square yard plot. Anyway, how big a house would a family of five people need? I bought the property at a price of ₹2,300 per square yard. That has appreciated to ₹5 lakh per square yard.

Now that I owned a house, I could at last acquire custom-built furniture for specific spaces and niches. In the years leading up to the purchase of my house in Safdarjung Enclave, I had had to make do with standard furniture that could fit into any house.

Meanwhile, Sandip enrolled for a B. Com degree at Bhagat Singh College in Delhi and joined HSIL soon after graduating. Remembering Jack Hay's comment that the ceramics and sanitaryware industry would yield profits only if there was proper supervision, I first put Sandip on the shopfloor to teach him the manufacturing process. If he could master the process as I had all those years ago, no one would be able to fool him in the future. I'm happy that he diligently learnt the trade and is now considered an expert in the field.

In January 1987, Sandip married Sumita, who is originally from Bombay. Her elder sister is my brother Surendra Kumar's wife, my bhabi. So we have a curious situation in our family, where two sisters are at the same time aunt-in-law and niece-in-law. That makes Bhabi my grandson Shashwat's great aunt as well as *mausi*, and Surendra Kumar's sons his uncles as well as cousins!

That's a recipe for confusion and an idea for a Bollywood comedy if ever there was one!

Sumita joined the family business three years ago and is in charge of Evok, our retail home-furnishings business as executive director.

Shashwat, who is currently pursuing his bachelor of business administration (BBA) at the University of California, Los Angeles, was born in 1995 and studied in Modern School. My grandson and I bond very closely. Like me and my son, he too loves cars and we often drive down to Sagar Ratna on Sundays for a south Indian meal over which we discuss various subjects, including his studies, technology, philosophy and business.

I have also learnt a lot from him and because of him. One day, he teasingly dubbed me 'tech unsavvy' because I hadn't yet converted to the cult of Apple.

I have always tried to learn new things and in fact, get restless if I don't pick up something new every few days. So at the age of nearly seventy, I taught myself to use a computer, became net-savvy and, a few years later, the first in the extended Somany clan to own an Apple iPhone 5.

Now, I use my iPhone to schedule and keep all my appointments and for various other requirements. I also read the daily reports I receive from my eight factories on my iPad. Not bad for a seventy-eight-year-old who didn't know how to use a computer less than a decade ago.

My elder daughter Sandhya studied B. Com at Jesus and Mary College in New Delhi. In 1992, I arranged her marriage to Arvind Agarwal, whose family had sold its tea business and entered the real- estate sector. Her son Udish is studying BBA in the US. Sandhya, like her mother Krishna, is an excellent cook and enjoys pottery and ikebana as hobbies.

Divya, too, studied B. Com at Jesus and Mary College and then followed this up with a Master's degree in sociology from Jawaharlal Nehru University. She married in 2001. Unfortunately, it lasted only three years. She now teaches at a leading school in New Delhi.

Tragedy struck my family again on 20 November 2000.

Snehlata, my third wife, who had done so much to stablize my family and had been such a good mother to my three children, died that day. Once again, fate ensured I couldn't be around when the end came.

I had left for Shanghai on business the previous day. She looked healthy except for an attack of cough and cold. At Shanghai, I received a message to call Bhaiji. I borrowed a phone from a supplier and called Ram Babu Kabra, president of HSIL, who told me: 'Sir, your wife has been admitted to Escorts Hospital.' He seemed reluctant to say anything beyond that.

My sixth sense warned me to expect the worst, but the human mind is inherently optimistic, so I continued to hope against hope.

I called up Abhishek, Bhaiji's grandson. 'Tell me the truth. How is Dadiji?' I asked him point blank, but didn't receive any conclusive reply.

I called my house. Sandhya answered the phone. She sounded shaken. Divya and Sumita, my daughter-in-law, were both with her. Escorts allowed one family member or attendant to stay with patients. What were all of them doing at home? I knew immediately that my sixth sense had been right.

She had no history of cardiac problems, yet her heart had failed her. She was only fifty-six. It was fate.

God was being unfair to me, I felt. How could I run my life?

The fact that I was a workaholic and maintained an eighteen-hour daily schedule helped me deal with my personal tragedies and get on with life.

My day begins at 6 a.m. every morning and my iPhone is filled with engagements, appointments, meetings and things to do till midnight.

I live in Delhi and work in Gurgaon. This means I often spend three to four hours in my car every day. I use this time to read reports or, sometimes, a book. In my younger days, I loved detective thrillers, but now, I mostly read autobiographies and management books and try to pick up tips on how to run my businesses more efficiently.

For me, office is a place of work and so I don't encourage social visits by friends and acquaintances. I abhor gossip and really don't have time for people who drop in just to say, 'this person is doing this', or 'do you know, that person is doing that'. Many people call me boring because of this, but I don't care.

Another thing I dislike is ostentation. I live simply, count my pennies and cut my coat according to my cloth. As I've said in the preceding pages, I lived in rented houses till I could afford to buy my own. I did so without taking any loans. In fact, I have no personal debts and take pride in the fact that I have repaid every single loan taken by my company before the due date.

My office room is relatively small. People have told me that divisional heads of comparable companies have larger cabins than mine. But what will I do with more space? Will it improve my efficiency? Will it make my company more profitable? It won't. I have never been able to find any merit in the arguments of people who say I should sit in a bigger cabin.

My food habits, likewise, are very simple—two *sabzis*, a small bowl of dal, one cucumber, one tomato, one thin roti and a bowl of yoghurt. I gave up eating papad a few years ago, just to test my will power. For a Marwari, to give up papad is like a Bengali giving up sweets or an alcoholic, his favourite drink. It is such an integral part of Marwari cuisine that many friends and relatives told me I wouldn't be able to sustain it for long. It has now been a full year since I gave up papad, but I've held firm.

I have never tasted alcohol in my life except once, when, on my seventy-fifth birthday, I had one sip of champagne. But I still maintain a bar at home. My son is an occasional drinker, but that isn't why I set it up.

On a few occasions, I found that some of my younger relatives and associates were declining my invitations. At first, I didn't think much about it but soon, a pattern began to emerge. Imagine my surprise when I discovered the reason: they didn't want to miss out on their evening tipple by coming home to dinner.

I don't have a moral issue with drinking. It's a social habit and its growing acceptance in our society is a sign of the times and I have always striven to keep up with changing tastes.

On Sundays, I make it a point to call up my brothers, sisters and Ganga Bhabi. All relationships are like finely tuned instruments, which need regular care and effort to nurture. I also make it a point to call them, as well as my close friends and business associates, on their birthdays and anniversaries. Smart phones and social media have made it a lot easier to remember these occasions.

I also make sure to give my two surviving sisters identical gifts for Rakshabandhan. I gives me great pleasure to know that they look forward to these small gifts, which are really only a token of my affection for them.

Everyone is busy with his or her own life. It is very easy to become disconnected from people close to you. Such small gestures keep relationships fresh and help renew ties.

8

GIVING BACK TO SOCIETY

I almost didn't become a member of Rotary Club. Inder Kumar Gujral, who was to become prime minister of India three decades later, in April 1997, had got me blackballed.

I was astounded when I heard the news. I didn't know Gujral personally. In fact, I didn't even know who he was. Gujral wasn't very prominent in those days, and would become a Congress Rajya Sabha member two years later in 1964. His brother Satish, an artist, was better known than he was.

As you know by now, when Krishna and I moved to Delhi in 1961, we didn't know anyone in the city. We had no relatives or friends in Delhi. After a few months, Krishna found out that her childhood friend from Calcutta, Saroj Sethia, whom she had lost touch with, was also in Delhi, having moved after marrying Nirmal Rakyan, who came from a family of leading jewellers in the city.

Connections were renewed and I became good friends with Nirmal. In fact, we joined Jaycees together. His father, Jawaharlal Rakyan, a prominent member of Delhi society, was a Rotarian. One evening, Saroj invited us to their home for dinner. Over the delicious spread that she laid out, her father-in-law started talking about the Rotary Club in which he was active.

What he said piqued my interest. I met him several times over the next months and heard more about the organization. He explained the various charitable and social services he was involved with on behalf of Rotary Club and offered to make me a member. That was in 1962.

The then president of the Delhi Rotary Club, R.N. Marwah, a chartered accountant, proposed my name. Jawaharlal Rakyan seconded me. Membership was now a mere formality, I was told.

Imagine my shock when three weeks later, I learnt that I had been blackballed. I didn't know anyone in the Rotary Club apart from Mr Marwah and Mr Rakyan. I knew very few people in Delhi and, to the best of my knowledge, had no enemies.

'Do you recall Gyanchand Vidyadhar?' Mr Rakyan asked a few days later. It was a small construction firm. The name meant nothing to me. I thought Bhaiji might know the firm, so the following morning, I placed a lightning call to him. The call came through by late afternoon. Those were the days before STD. Long-distance phone calls, called trunk calls, had to be booked through an operator at the telephone exchange and one had to wait for hours before one got to speak to the called party.

The name didn't ring a bell for Bhaiji, who had started building the factory while I was in England. 'I'd given one contract for the construction of the warehouse but don't recall the name of the contractor,' he said.

I put Dev, my secretary, to work, sifting through old files to check if we had had any dealings with this firm. The eureka moment came a few hours later, when Dev located a file which showed that Gyanchand Vidyadhar was indeed the contractor my brother had retained to build the warehouse. But the firm had abandoned the work without any intimation to us following a massive flood in the area in which my factory was located, causing some delay in its construction and a fair bit of inconvenience to us. The firm had left behind some material and equipment at the factory site, which it had not claimed.

I.K. Gujral, it seems, had a stake in the firm.

'Are you willing to settle?' Mr Rakyan asked.

I said I was.

'Bring your chequebook,' he said.

A meeting was set up between the managing partner of the firm, a Mr Batra, and me in the backyard of Mr Rakyan's showroom on Janpath on a Sunday morning. There, sitting on a charpoy, I negotiated a settlement of ₹20,000 for his abandoned material and equipment.

There was another reason for blackballing me. The Rotary Club had two factions—one headed by Mr Gujral and the other led by Mr Marwah and Mr Rakyan. A member proposed by the Gujral faction had been rejected. So they got their revenge by blocking my entry.

Now that the cause of friction was out of the way, I presumed that I would be admitted into the Rotary Club. But there was a rule that a blackballed candidate would have to wait for a year before his application could be considered again.

A few years after this incident, Mr Gujral called me early one morning. His brother Satish had won the contract to do the facade of Odeon Cinema in Connaught Place. But the work had ground to a halt as the kiln in which he was firing the ceramic tiles needed for his work had broken down.

'Can you help out, please?' he asked.

I did and the work resumed.

I was finally inducted into the Rotary Club a year after I was blackballed, on 18 April 1963. The club held its meetings at the Imperial Hotel Ballroom every Wednesday. These were boring, desultory affairs. Only fifteen or twenty of the 250-odd members would attend. Often, visiting members would outnumber us.

Our chapter of the Rotary, I soon discovered, was plagued with intense factionalism, of which I had been a victim at the time of joining. Young members were not given a chance to speak their minds and the club wasn't really fulfilling its charter of trying to improve society. There was simmering discontent among a large body of members, but no one dared to speak out because of the stature and influence of the senior members who were at the helm.

Finally, some of us decided to form the Rotary Club of Delhi Midtown as a separate Luncheon Club within the same Rotary district in 1974. This new club became District 3010 and later, District 3011.

We got our charter on 18 March 1975. Unfortunately, I couldn't sign it as I was travelling, I am therefore, not a charter member. But I have been a member since the day the club was formed. We would meet for lunch every Friday at the Oberoi Hotel.

Having seen first hand how factionalism could debilitate the functioning of the club, we decided that office bearers would be selected by a nomination committee, instead of the usual process of holding elections. We had experienced from close quarters how the election of a president from one faction and the secretary from another could paralyse decision-making.

Under the new system, the president could choose his own team and thus create a cohesive leadership team that could then carry out its designated tasks. Every president has a one-year term and all projects conceived by him have to be completed within his term. If a project is for a longer term, the next two presidents have to agree to it so as to get a buy-in for the future.

We carried out several charitable and social activities, including organizing regular blood-donation camps. One of our members was hearing challenged. This gave me an idea. I proposed donating hearing aids to children who were hearing challenged. The proposal was accepted and we gave away fifty such instruments to children of a local school. They came to thank us; their expressions of gratitude were very moving and heart-warming. I felt tears rolling down my cheeks.

I became the sixth president of the Luncheon Club in 1980–81 and then joined its board as a past president. Thirty-five years later, I continue to be associated with the organization.

I have touched briefly on my association with the Jaycees in a previous chapter. Nirmal Rakyan and I joined the organization together in 1964. It wasn't very active at the time. It had about thirty members drawn from all walks of life. Wives were often invited to the meetings, which were held at Ashoka Hotel, sometimes over high tea, sometimes over dinner. That is how our friends' circle grew.

It was an excellent training ground for young leaders, especially in public speaking and on conducting meetings. It was during my association with the Jaycees that I was introduced to Robert's *Rule of Order*. The book is a bible on how to conduct meetings. Chambers of commerce assume that members know these things, but I can say from experience that many people don't. Formally training young people in this field could make chamber and corporate meetings more meaningful and productive.

The Jaycees also engaged in community service. In 1967, I had the honour of visiting Indira Gandhi at the prime minister's residence. She gave away fifty wheelchairs the Jaycees had donated to handicapped people. We also organized several blood-donation camps in collaboration with the Indian Red Cross Society as well as a few eye operation camps.

Those were the days when India was considered by the western media as the sick man of Asia. Two hundred years of colonialism and systematic officially sanctioned economic plunder had sapped India's strength and left the country, the world's richest when the British took over, as miserably poor. Following Independence, the socialist model of development adopted by the Jawaharlal Nehru government had impeded any chance of recovery.

As a result, India was groaning under the weight of its economic misfortune. Two successive years of droughts in the mid-1960s had created famine-like conditions in large parts of the country, forcing the government to approach the United States for food aid under its Public Law 480 provisions. But India's request for food aid was accompanied by high-pitched criticism of the United States' actions in Vietnam, which infuriated the administration and lawmakers in that country. The resulting diplomatic face-off led to shrill calls from influential sections of society to withdraw our request for food aid.

But Indira Gandhi reportedly dismissed this demand saying: 'Nothing will happen to them if the US stops food shipments. Only the poor will suffer.'

Thus, it came about that Indians had to live, what the

condescending western media pejoratively dubbed, 'from ship to mouth'.

With food shortages all around, it was a sin to waste even a grain. In response, the Jaycees, of which I was then the president, launched the 'waste not, want not' campaign to encourage people not to waste any food on their plates. It was admittedly not a mass campaign. The Jaycees was too small an organization for that. But it was well received in the corporate circles in which we propagated it. I am happy that we were able to contribute—even though it was just a drop in the ocean—at a time of dire need.

Even now, I make it a point to ensure that my plate is completely clean when I finish my meals. My grandson Shashwat, I'm happy to report, has inculcated this habit and ensures that he never wastes a morsel of food.

I made several lifelong friends at the Jaycees, among them Shashi Budhiraja, who was working with Burma Shell at the time, and Binay Kumar, the owner of Benaras House, a large export firm. Budhiraja, who later became managing director of Indian Oil Corporation, and Kumar both served on the board of HSIL as directors. They retired recently after they crossed eighty as I needed to induct younger blood on the board, but both of them remain my good friends.

Through the Jaycees, I was able to meet people from varied backgrounds. Pramod Malhotra, another friend I made at the Jaycees, worked for Citibank; Vinod Mehta and Gulshan Rai were chartered accountants; F.C. Pahwa a government servant and Suresh Shangle an LIC agent. Amin Sayani, who is called the Golden Voice of Indian Radio, was also a member of the Jaycees. I met him in Ranchi in the 1960s.

My association with the Jaycees also had an unexpected result.

Sir Udayan Chinubhai, Third Baronet of Shahpur, was national president of the organization in 1962. His daughter was suggested as a match for my nephew Arvind, Surendra Kumar's son. When the two families met, Sir Udayan said: 'I know one Rajendra Somany.' The marriage was sealed without further ado.

I retired from the Jaycees in 1967 after serving my term as president, as my business was growing and needed more attention and also because I had joined the Rotary Club by then.

I joined the Punjab, Haryana and Delhi Chamber of Commerce and Industries (PHDCCI) in 1970. L.M. Thapar, one of India's leading industrialists and a towering personality, was its president at the time.

My stint at the Jaycees had taught me the importance of reading the by-laws of an organization before attending meetings. One day, I stood up and told Mr Thapar: 'Mr President, according to the rules, you need to add a new member to the governing council for every so many additional general body members...'

A quick perusal of the rule book showed I was correct.

'But we have no space,' replied Mr Thapar. Taking on a new member in the governing council would require additional office space and new seating arrangements. PHDCCI then had its office in the Phelps Building in Connaught Place, a cramped space that was clearly insufficient for the work it did.

'Let us apply for land,' I responded.

Our application for land was soon approved by the government and we built a large office in keeping with PHDCCI's position as the capital's leading chamber of commerce. The terms of allotment, however, specifically precluded renting out space in the premises for offices or other establishments, thus depriving the chamber of an important potential, and much-needed, revenue stream. We got around this problem by renting out space on a temporary basis for exhibitions, conventions and other meetings. Such spaces were not easily available in Delhi at the time. This gave PHDCCI a regular source of income and helped pay off the loans it had taken for the construction of the office.

In those days, the president had to be elected, unlike now, when the vice president of PHDCCI is automatically elevated to the top post when the incumbent president completes his term.

When it was my turn to contest for the president's post, I.P. Anand, a senior and respected member of the chamber, requested me to stand aside in favour of a gentleman who had contested several times and lost on every occasion. 'You can wait for a year,' he said.

The gentleman in question was a senior and respected member of the chamber, so I complied with Mr Anand's appeal. But the gentleman lost the election yet again. A sheepish-looking Mr Anand told me very apologetically: 'Sorry, Somanyji...'

I finally became president of PHDCCI in 1989–90. M.M. Sabharwal, former managing director of Dunlop, was president before me. He was a well-known management expert, a thorough gentleman and a top-class professional. I learnt a lot from him.

My association with PHDCCI offered me a chance to do something I had wanted to for a long time—visit Pakistan. I had heard a lot about that country from Bhaiji, who had visited Lahore and Karachi several times before Independence. As I have mentioned, we used to control more than 90 per cent of the jute market in the northwest of India prior to 1947.

I finally got the chance in 1982, when V.P. Punj, of the Punj Llyod Group, was president of PHDCCI. N. Nandajog, secretary general of PHDCCI, called one Thursday and said: 'Somanyji, send me your passport. We're leaving for Pakistan on Saturday.'

Bhaiji, who I consulted on most matters, told me to go ahead and make the trip.

I had a few very mundane concerns. I am a vegetarian. Would they serve vegetarian food there? What would I eat? To be safe, I decided to carry some food with me.

S.P. Oswal of the Oswal Group, and B.M. Munjal of Hero Honda Motors (now Hero Motocorp) were also part of the delegation.

In Lahore, a well-dressed young man, who introduced himself as the owner of a local company called International Ceramics, came to see me.

'Why don't you visit our factory?' he said.

His factory used gas as a fuel. I asked him the price of gas and whether it was cheaper to operate the plant on gas or electricity. He had no idea. He couldn't answer a few other basic questions on costs and technology.

'My wife had gone to Delhi a few years ago. She saw an HSIL water closet in a showroom in Connaught Place and wanted one like it. When I made enquiries here, I found the margins were massive—anywhere between 200 per cent and 400 per cent. So, I set up the factory. Input costs don't really matter,' he said by way of explanation.

My interest piqued, I visited the local markets and made enquiries. Sure enough, American Standard, Kohler and other international brands were selling their products with 200 to 400 per cent profit margins. I was astonished to find HSIL products on display as well—at prices well above what I was getting in India.

I happened to know the Pakistani commercial secretary attached to the high commission in Delhi, as he lived close to our house in Vasant Vihar, where I had moved into another rented house.

BRINGING THE RAINBOW

He had told me that there was a huge demand for my products in Pakistan and that they were being smuggled across the border near Amritsar and sold at a huge premium. The evidence before my eyes confirmed what he had said.

Ruminating further on the issue, I figured it made sense. Pakistan had, for a while earlier, allowed imports of ceramic sanitaryware from India. At the time, Pakistani traders would visit our Bahadurgarh plant and buy wagonloads of my products. The clamping down on legal imports had simply driven this trade underground. But as long as demand existed, people would find a way to meet it. I pondered for a while on the opportunities and profits HSIL had had to forego because of the political and diplomatic problems between our two countries.

Our trip to Pakistan also included visits to Islamabad, Lahore and Karachi. We were at the Islamabad airport on our way to Karachi. The Pakistan International Airlines flight had been delayed. Mr Punj, with whom I had been chatting, was tired. Leaving him to get some rest, I headed for the washroom. Imagine my surprise and pride when I saw that every single sanitaryware item was a Hindware product. I have no idea how they were procured. They had obviously been smuggled into Pakistan. But to find smuggled products in a government-owned facility in the Pakistani capital was both a cause for shock and delight.

In Karachi, as in Lahore and Islamabad, the hospitality was warm and overwhelming. Our hosts went out of their way to make us feel at home. A leading Sindhi business family, among the richest in Pakistan, invited us for dinner. The house was imposingly large and luxurious, with high walls maintaining the privacy and security of its inhabitants.

The reception was as grand as any I have attended anywhere

in the world. Alcohol of every description and brand was flowing like water. And yes, in addition to the eye-popping amounts of non-vegetarian fare, there was also a wide assortment of vegetarian food for people like me.

Our host had invited hundreds of people—including the leading lights of the government—to the reception. None of them seemed to mind the flowing liquor, though Pakistan is officially an Islamic state where alcohol is taboo. It seemed as if the laws of the land didn't apply to the rich and the powerful. At least in this one respect, our two countries are very alike. Common DNA, some would say.

A few years later, I visited Kenya and Tanzania on a family vacation. We stopped at a petrol station to refuel our car. I went to the washroom and found Hindware products there. The basin and the water closet were dirty and badly maintained, but I felt proud.

Apart from various chambers of commerce, I have also been associated with various social organizations. My experiences there have taught me that even small institutional interventions can bring about big changes in the lives of individuals.

Soon after the horrifying gang rape of a young woman in Delhi on 16 December 2012, which was dubbed the 'Nirbhaya Case' by the media, I noticed a group of women colleagues leaving the HSIL office after dusk.

A thought struck me. Many of these women used public transport and would have to walk home alone from bus stops and metro stations. The rising number of crimes against women meant all of them were exposing themselves to some degree of risk on their way back from work. Though their safety outside office was not our responsibility, I felt we should do something about it.

I called the head of human resources at HSIL and asked: 'How many women work in HSIL?'

It turned out that 57 out of 180 staff members at our Gurgaon corporate office were women.

'Let us organize self-defence training for them,' I said.

Over the next four weekends, we hired certified self-defence trainers to conduct such a course for HSIL's women employees. We did the same at our plant in Bahadurgarh.

A few of the women emailed me, thanking me for the initiative, saying the self-defence workshops had boosted their confidence.

I felt good.

I am also associated with another, much bigger, institutional initiative that can potentially change millions of lives.

Many organizations such as the World Bank, the International Monetary Fund (IMF) and large sections of global and domestic industry believe India is on the cusp of an economic revolution that can permanently release its 1.25 billion citizens from the curse of unemployment and low productivity and lead them to prosperity.

Every year, twelve to fifteen million young men and women join the country's workforce. Finding employment for them is a Herculean task. The problem is that the majority of them do not have any employable skills. Our education system does nothing to improve employability. In any case, a majority of this vast army of youngsters lacks formal education.

The way out of this problem is to train them in skills that will ensure jobs and livelihoods. The government has launched an initiative in this regard and entrusted the job of re-skilling India to the National Skills Development Council (NSDC), which is a public-private initiative. The government owns 49 per cent of the ₹10-crore equity in this not-for-profit company, while the balance is owned equally by the Confederation of Indian Industry (CII), Federation of Indian Chambers of Commerce and Industry (FICCI) and the Associated Chambers of Commerce (ASSOCHAM), the three apex chambers of commerce in India.

One small part of this initiative involves training 1.2 million plumbers. This task has been entrusted to the Indian Plumbing Skills Council (IPSC). A senior office bearer of NSDC called me one day in 2012 and asked me to become the first chairman of IPSC. As I had been involved with the sanitaryware and bathroom-fittings industry for five-and-a-half decades, and HSIL is the largest company in this segment NSDC probably felt I would be a good choice to head IPSC—almost by default, as it were.

I had been grappling with the issue of training plumbers for a long time. There was, till IPSC took up the task, no system of certifying plumbers. When people buy plumbing and sanitaryware products, which are often expensive, they expect people with a minimum level of competence and training to fit them. Currently, that is completely a matter of chance. If they are lucky, they will find someone competent enough to do a proper job of installing the products. If they are not, their plumbing products could be damaged.

HSIL employs three hundred plumbers and supervisors on contract to undertake plumbing work. We train them to fit and service our products, some of which, especially at the top end, are quite high tech.

About eight years ago, a friend called to say his plumber had damaged a high-end bathroom fitting he had wanted fitted in his bathroom and sought my help to fix it. I couldn't help out as the product was that of a competing brand, but that set me thinking. Should we start servicing other companies' products?

The IPSC training module offers a solution to this problem. But more importantly, it provides hope for generating sustainable livelihoods for about six million people, assuming that one working individual supports a family of five.

The training is outsourced, on the basis of a standard curriculum devised by IPSC, to affiliated partners across the country. We then send assessors to conduct due diligence on their performance and issue certificates to plumbers who successfully complete the programme.

'About 90 per cent of the plumbing industry workforce in India is not professionally trained. Most of the skill learning in the industry happens through unstructured on-the-job training. Lack of professionally trained plumbers is a major drawback for the country's construction and related sector. The IPSC will endeavour to address these issues and bring the skill levels in our country to world standards,' I wrote in a letter that has been put up on the IPSC website.

I have also been associated with industry bodies such as ASSOCHAM and Employers' Federation of India (EFI).

The former was considered an association for foreign companies operating in India. Like most Indian business houses, the undivided Somany Group, comprising HNG, HSIL, Somany Pilkington, Soma Textiles and their affiliates, had been members of FICCI, the 'nationalist business chamber' established in 1927 by G.D. Birla and Purushottam Das Thakurdas on the advice of Mahatma Gandhi, to give voice to Indian-owned industry. ASSOCHAM, the leading chamber of commerce in India before the advent of FICCI, was dominated by British-owned companies and so wasn't considered sympathetic to the needs of their Indian-owned rivals.

When the controversy over fake members led to FICCI stalwarts such as Hari Shankar Singhania, L.M. Thapar, Bhaiji and others leaving it and joining ASSOCHAM, I wasn't very keen on following suit. But Mr Singhania contacted me and convinced me to change my mind.

The chamber was almost bankrupt at the time, but its fortunes revived with the patronage of so many stalwarts of Indian industry. I joined as a member in 1985 and became its president in 2002. During my tenure at the helm of ASSOCHAM, we organized a two-and-a-half day conference on the 'Business of Biotechnology', which was inaugurated by the then President of India, Dr A.P.J. Abdul Kalam.

The Employers Federation of India (EFI) is a body of some of India's leading industrialists registered, ironically, under the Trade Union Act, and has its registered office in Mumbai. Doyens of industry such as Naval Tata and Keshav Mahindra have been presidents of EFI.

My involvement with EFI began on a slightly strange note. When I was asked to chair the Human Resource & Industrial Relations (HRIR) committee, they asked me to chair the EFI Delhi Chapter as well. I wasn't then a member of EFI and said my conscience wouldn't allow me to take up the responsibility. So I became a member. Though it was a national body, I found that it was basically a club of Bombay industrialists and fought tooth and nail to make it truly national by encouraging it to take in members from other cities and regions.

I probably inherited my desire to give back to society from my ancestors. My grandfather Ram Prasad Somany, who had gone to Calcutta more than a century ago to seek out his fortune, had been a public-spirited individual, who, like many other Marwari businessmen, had generously opened his purse strings in pursuit of public good. The school he established in Chirawa in 1915 celebrated its centenary in 2015 and is still run by trusts controlled by my family.

I have, in my own humble way, tried to continue the tradition of sharing my family's good fortune with those sections of society that need support. With this in mind, I had set up the Krishna Somany Charity Trust in the memory of my wife and built an orphanage in Bahadurgarh in 2015. I used my personal money for the purpose. Recently, the orphanage expanded its capacity by building a first floor with a contribution from HSIL's corporate social responsibility (CSR) funds. I have also used a part of HSIL's CSR corpus to build many check dams in the Alwar district in Rajasthan to facilitate the storage of rain water in the area.

The government has launched a commendable initiative to build millions of toilets across India under the Swachh Bharat Abhiyan. Having experienced first hand the problems associated with open defecation at my native place in Chirawa—and given the rising graph of crimes against women—this programme hasn't come a day too soon.

The scheme is not only expected to encourage personal hygiene among Indians, it is also likely to lead to higher enrolment rates and lower dropout rates at rural girls' schools, as many students stay away from schools because they lack toilets.

HSIL has taken upon itself the responsibility of building fifty such toilets in Bhiwadi, Rajasthan but we have faced a few issues relating to quality of work, maintenance and monitoring, as well as a few local problems. Hopefully, these will get sorted out soon and we will be able to complete our work without too much delay.

I am happy to report that other CSR initiatives such as providing tailoring training to women, providing basic computer literacy, setting up an OPD centre and a scheme to provide drinking water are up and running, and contributing to enriching the lives of the people in the local communities in which we operate.

I now devote 50 per cent of my time to pro-bono work. My involvement with such work comes from a deep commitment to try and make a difference to society and a belief that every individual should try and leave the world a better place than the one he or she came into. These sentiments draw deeply from my Marwari ethos, which has contributed so much to philanthropy and the spirit of giving in India.

God has been kind to me. My company is doing well and over the years, my son Sandip has taken over a lot of my work, leaving me with more time to spare for work that gives me as much pleasure as my business. It is my humble way of saying thank you to God and country.

9

FROM NEWBIE TO MARKET LEADER

Hindusthan Twyfords was the new kid on the block when we started out. But as I've said in previous chapters, we hit a market plagued with shortages with a product years ahead of its time. This allowed me to go from new kid on the block to market leader with relative ease.

Nothing illustrates this better than an incident that took place soon after HTL started production. Bhaiji, who was the founder chairman of the company, called me from Chennai. 'I'm talking to about sixty dealers here. They want to see the quality of our products.'

We were the first to introduce vitreous china products in the country. Imports of sanitaryware had been stopped to conserve precious foreign exchange. Our competitors were selling earthenware products that absorbed water when they chipped, as such items were wont to do. The dealers wanted to see for themselves if HTL products were really different and superior as we claimed.

I sent a selection of our products to Bhaiji. The dealers couldn't believe that the basins, water closets and Indian-style pans had been made in India. 'We don't believe you could have made these in India. You have imported them from your British collaborator,' they said.

Meanwhile, as word spread that HTL was about to start production, we began getting lots of calls from many influential people in Delhi and Mumbai asking for sole selling agencies in different regions. Bawa Bachittar Singh was then the mayor of Delhi. He called me one day to ask for an exclusive agency. 'You don't understand marketing,' he said. 'You'll lose your shirt.'

There were a few other such calls as well, all from influential people and established dealers. I wasn't comfortable with the idea of giving them sole selling agencies as this would place us, the manufacturer, completely at their mercy.

It was a seller's market when we entered the industry as there was a complete absence of good-quality sanitaryware. It was standard practice for dealers to visit the offices of the existing companies to grease the palms of executives to get their quotas. Given the acute shortage in the market, they would then sell to the end users at a premium—in the black market.

'They'll squeeze the marrow out of the bone,' I told Bhaiji. He concurred.

Our products were far superior to anything else in the market and were thus expected to command a higher premium than the competition. This was prompting the rash of enquiries.

I appointed two independent dealers in Delhi—Gurbax Singh & Sons on Asaf Ali Road and Mahavir Parshad in Chowri Bazar—and made R.B. Rodda & Co, which had a presence in Delhi as well, my third dealer in the capital. I also appointed one dealer each in Ranchi and Kanpur, and two each in Calcutta and Mumbai and then, over the years, gradually expanded the network.

HTL quickly established a reputation for producing high-quality products at prices that customers considered fair. Earlier, sanitaryware was mainly purchased by contractors and plumbers, not by householders and business establishments, as there wasn't much differentiation and the products, even those produced by competing companies, were similar in most aspects.

Our entry into the market changed that. For the first time since imports had been banned, consumers were actually asking for, and buying, a particular brand of sanitaryware—ours. The glaze, shine, finish and elegant designs were the draws. In such a situation, it wasn't surprising that we started receiving dozens of applications for dealerships.

I was clear in my mind that I wouldn't give away dealerships like candy. I put in place strong systems to screen potential dealers and conducted very rigorous due diligence before signing them up. There was sound business logic for this: for consumers, dealers are the front end of the company. End users never meet any HTL executives. They only interact with dealers. I wanted this interface to be as comfortable and seamless as possible. This is now considered the ABC of marketing, but fifty years ago, this was a revolutionary step and I can say with pride that HTL's initiatives so many decades ago helped transform the sanitaryware market from a commodity business to one where brands, including the leading ones from the West, dominate.

I have always been very hands-on in whatever I do. I had mastered the art and science of manufacturing sanitaryware the hard way—by working on the shop floor of the Twyfords factory in

England. But I was still a newbie in the market. To succeed, it was important to receive frank and honest feedback from the ground. I didn't want to depend solely on dealer feedback for this. So, I started going on field trips to familiarize myself with the market. I would meet not only my own dealers but also visit the dealers of my rivals to find out first hand about market trends and demand.

I was particularly keen on finding out about the problems they faced—from sourcing our products, transporting them, storing them and selling them. The feedback I received was critical, especially in the early days, and enabled me to understand the entire supply chain without which it would have been impossible to succeed.

Even now, I still meet dealers, though not as regularly as I used to, to enquire about the problems they face. Many of my peers, both in my own industry as well as in others, consider this a waste of time, preferring, instead, to leave this 'drudge work' to executives several levels below. I strongly disagree with this approach. It is important for top management to know the nuts and bolts of their trade. Without such first-hand knowledge, top management will find it extremely difficult to sail through difficult periods.

At HSIL, as in many other companies, we have strict protocols in place for appointing dealers. Our dealers' agreement template dates back to the era prior to the Monopolies & Restrictive Trade Practices Act, the passage of which made many of the clauses irrelevant. We have since amended the template according to the new laws. However, one clause that has remained unchanged for fifty-two years is the one on not allowing dealers to charge more than the maximum retail price—a clause we introduced decades before it became mandatory. This ensured that HSIL products could never be sold on the black market—a huge step in an age when almost every good product commanded a black-market premium and one be sold on the black market—a huge step in an age when almost every good product commanded a black-market premium and one which, I believe, enabled HSIL products to earn the goodwill of consumers across India.

As chairman of my company, I have always believed in ethical business practices and fair competition. Indulging in anti-competitive practices is not permitted and I follow a zero tolerance policy on this. Any dealer or distributor indulging in unethical trade practice is dealt with sternly.

On one occasion, a group of dealers from Kochi (Cochin) threatened to boycott our products if certain conditions were not met. I sent a very strong reply; that was the last we heard of those demands.

It is very difficult to remain the market leader and continue to make profits year after year for more than half a century. To do so, one has to ensure complete control over the entire value and supply chains, from casting to the final delivery of the finished product to the end user.

I have always tried to ensure this, even if it meant fighting, or severing ties, with those parts of the chain that were not in sync with the rest. As the person sitting at the apex of these two chains, I consider it my duty to ensure that all the constituent parts work in tandem and in harmony with each other—even if it calls for ruthless action from time to time. The entire edifice can come crumbling down if I display any laxity on this count.

I can say with pride that HSIL still remains the undisputed leader in the sanitaryware market despite the entry of the major global brands such as Roca, Kohler, Duravit, and others. I don't think we could have done this and held our own if we hadn't institutionalized the process of collecting and acting upon the ground-up feedback that we receive. It's common sense that you have to know your market and your customer.

To come back to the beginning, HTL began with washbasins in three sizes, an Indian pan, a western pan and an Orissa pan. G.L. Mehta, chairman of ICICI and ex-ambassador to United States, did the first casting for us, pouring the prepared liquid raw materials from a bucket into a cast.

In those days, it took about seventeen days from the day we poured the liquid into the cast to the day the finished product was despatched to the warehouse. It wasn't an entirely smooth run and we had to innovate on the fly to overcome the issues we faced in the initial days.

Our collaborator hadn't informed us about the need for environment control. To ensure flawless products, it was imperative to maintain a certain level of moisture in the system. This was not an issue in England but could seriously impact the quality of output in the hot and dry north Indian climate. We overcame this by simply spraying water into the system.

Then, the kilns use indirect heating leading to massive loss of energy. We used low-sulphur high-stock (LSHS) light diesel oil and furnace oil as fuel. All of these have a high sulphur content and are dangerous for human beings. When we cleaned the kilns, we had to dispose of humungous amounts of sulphur powder.

We began by producing only sixty units per day. There wasn't much competition and we managed to sell this production very easily. But this kind of batch production was not conducive to building up volumes. The market was eagerly lapping up our products, but we lacked the capacity to match this demand with supply.

In January–February 1963, we introduced a tunnel kiln, which allowed continuous production. This gave us a loading capacity of 450–500 pieces a day and also reduced the production process to twenty-nine hours. In December that year, we installed a 405-foot-long tunnel kiln that increased output by 900–1,000 pieces a day, giving us a total production of about 1,500 pieces.

As I've mentioned earlier, as our capacity and production increased, economies of scale reduced our cost of production considerably, allowing us to pass on the benefits of reduced prices, thus creating a better value proposition for customers.

This combination of superior products and sharply lower prices gave us an unbeatable advantage in the market and enabled us to quickly gain market leadership—a position we have retained for more than half a century. Today, HSIL commands a 40 per cent share of the market and is the leading brand of sanitaryware in India by a long distance.

Our association with Twyfords ended after three years as per our contract, but it retained its shareholding till 2008. Following the end of the collaboration, Hindusthan Twyfords changed its name to Hindustan Sanitaryware and Industries Ltd. Many years later, this was shortened to HSIL, the acronym by which we were known in the market.

When we started out, Twyfords had sent six expatriates to work in India. They held critical positions in the technical and production side of the business and their support was vital to establishing the company and the brand. Importantly, they also trained our workers, many of whom were working in a large factory for the first time.

We soon internalized the technology and the processes and the expatriate managers began to leave by the end of the second year of the partnership. Only Reg Hancock, with whom I had struck up a friendship in England, stayed on till the end of the three years, working as the head of the plant. Another expat, W.C. Hancock (no relation to Reg) came later and worked for two years to improve the efficiency of the casting shop.

Unwittingly, the actions of these expatriate managers brought me face to face with the first major crisis of my then fledgling career as a young industrialist. The first labour strike at HTL took place in 1965–66. Till then, the company had functioned smoothly, producing ever-increasing volumes of quality sanitaryware that we shipped out to dealerships around the country.

In England, there is not much difference between supervisors and workers. They often come from similar backgrounds, go drinking at the same pubs and socialize with each other. There is little apparent class difference and this helps maintain harmony and industrial peace.

In India, we have a very hierarchical society and promoting one person and not his neighbour can play havoc with existing social hierarchies and lead to tensions.

Reg Hancock, unaware of these social nuances and going solely by merit, had appointed some workers as supervisors. This led to discontent among other workers. Since we were the only factory in the area, lots of outside labour leaders, eager to make a name for themselves, got involved. They incited the workers, made tall promises, cast us as villains and sold utopian dreams. Many of our workers fell prey to their incitement and blandishments. Workers affiliated to the Indian National Trade Union Congress, the trade union wing of the Indian National Congress, threatened to go on strike and then actually struck work.

This was my first experience of industrial action by workers, but I was unfazed. I had been scrupulously fair to all stakeholders, including my workers, and didn't want to give in to this kind of blackmail. It was a matter of principle.

The strike lasted about thirty days, but in the end, the issues raised were amicably resolved. I increased wages but didn't concede much else.

The last strike we had was in 2004. Many of our older workers had children who were of working age and were pursuing their own professions. This gave the workers the financial wherewithal to embark on a longer strike and endure a longer period without wages. I realized this and allowed the strike to linger in order to wear them out.

Once again, outsiders and leaders of rival unions tried to get involved in order to expand their spheres of influence. This time, the strike lasted almost two months. There were no real issues that were at stake. Fortunately, the workers realized that they were being misled by their leaders and came back to work. We told them: 'What purpose does bringing in outsiders serve? They just flare things up, push their own agendas and go away once their goals are achieved, regardless of whether the workers get their way.' My workers understood this. Incredibly, the HSIL factory in Bahadurgarh no longer has a workers' union.

Meanwhile, we learnt about the market as we went along. India was still not very industrialized when we floated HTL and there was very little market intelligence and data to base decisions on. Often, I had to take decisions purely on intuition. Fortunately, my instincts proved right more often than not.

The situation is very different now. There are multiple sources of data; listed companies have to divulge information to the stock markets, which makes it possible to arrive at more scientific and reasoned decisions.

That wasn't the only issue in the early days. I started with about thirty executives and 110 workers. The office was located in the plant itself. It wasn't much of an office, really—with asbestos sheets for a roof, no air-conditioners, no fans, even. But the excitement of building something from scratch enabled all of us to overcome these difficulties. Life was much simpler in those days. I can't imagine any scion of a privileged family going through similar pain today.

It may intrigue readers to learn that though I have built and run HSIL from the very beginning, I wasn't a member of its board of directors for a long time. Though I was the de facto managing director of the company, I held the somewhat humble designation of production organizer. I remember being unhappy with the designation when Onkar Bhaiji first offered it to me. 'When Chandra Kumar joined HNG, he did so with the same designation. How can your designation be different?' he reasoned. I wasn't happy, but accepted his logic.

It was much later, in February 1974, that I was 'promoted' from production organizer to president. In 1988, I was appointed additional director and wholetime director. I became managing director in 1993 and the following year was appointed chairman and managing director.

By the late 1970s, HSIL was doing very well, earning profits, which were growing every year. We were also paying a huge amount in taxes and were looking for ways to lower the tax burden. One way of doing this was to buy a sick unit and set off its losses against the company profits and thus reduce the tax outflow.

In 1981, we zeroed in on AGI, a sick glass unit in Hyderabad. HNG had, by this time, emerged as the market leader in the glass bottles market, so the technology and the expertise required to turn AGI around was available within the family.

I had no experience of running a glass plant, so it fell upon Chandra Kumar, who was running HNG, to provide the expertise needed to turn AGI, which was a strategic business unit of HSIL, around. Additionally, Bhaiji's son Shreekant was sent to Hyderabad for a couple of years to manage the affairs of AGI with guidance from Chandra Kumar and under my supervision. I am happy to report that AGI today is profitable and continues to remain under my control as a division of HSIL.

As we were the market leader in the sanitaryware industry, I naturally kept a close watch on allied sectors such as bathroom fittings. In the 1980s, there was a dire need in the market for good-quality bathroom fittings. Having emerged as the leader in the glass (HNG) and sanitaryware (HSIL) industries, the family was exploring options to expand its horizons and capture other unconquered spaces. Hoping to recreate the magic of HSIL in the bathroom-fittings space, we set up Soma Plumbing. We leased a plot of industrial land in Sahibabad in Uttar Pradesh.

I was clear from the beginning—I would offer customers the same value proposition that had allowed HSIL to become a market leader. That meant obtaining the latest technology and designs available in the world.

After making enquiries in several countries, we identified a family-owned Swiss company called Similor SA, which was based in Geneva. It had a good reputation, excellent technology and very contemporary designs. Following a few rounds of negotiations, we bought Similor's technology and plant design for Swiss Franc5,000. The company also agreed to train my nephew Shreekant and an executive called Ganguly at its plant in Switzerland on the use of its technology.

This was the first time since setting up the Bahadurgarh plant of

HTL (which had by then been renamed HSIL) that I was setting up a company from scratch. In keeping with my experience at HSIL, we bought sophisticated machines, some of which, unfortunately, were never used. Perhaps, in retrospect, we over invested in this facility.

We started production, but our products and the technology we employed were far ahead of their time for the Indian market. For example, we introduced a tap with a non-rising spindle. We didn't invest in training plumbers, who, I learnt to my cost, could make or break a brand. They had no idea how to fix or repair our products and would often end up ruining them. As a result, customer experience was not up to the mark, sales suffered and losses mounted. That plant never achieved capacities to break even.

There were other problems as well. The factory was located in Uttar Pradesh (UP), which created its own set of problems. The power situation was precarious. We received barely four hours of supply a day from the grid. That meant we had to depend on a diesel generator, which was a very expensive proposition that played havoc with our costing.

Corruption was rampant. The 'inspector raj' was at its peak and sales tax and excise inspectors were constantly hounding us. Transporting goods across the Delhi-UP border meant we had to pay octroi tax. Local officials would stop our trucks for no reason and demand hefty bribes. The problem was accentuated because this was then mostly a cash business where buyers didn't bother about bills.

Losses mounted and we decided to send Shreekant, who was looking after the business, to Hyderabad to run AGI. I took direct charge of Soma Plumbing after that and put in systems to try and bring the business on track, but the writing was clearly visible on the wall.

Soma Plumbing wasn't going anywhere.

I told my brothers: 'You have to take a call on shutting it down.' I was particularly concerned as the company was a 100 per cent subsidiary of HSIL and its non-performance was proving to be a drag on the functioning of the parent company.

Bhaiji was very annoyed. We had invested a fair amount of money and also put the reputation of the Somany family at stake. Failure to make a success of the venture could have unforeseen repercussions, but I refused to run the company any more. Following a few more not-so-pleasant encounters with my brothers, we finally decided to cut our losses and shut down the company.

I liquidated Soma Plumbing machine by machine—some of which I sold as scrap—returned the land to the UP government and wound up the business. This was the first failed project of HSIL, which was then more than a quarter of a century old at the time.

The only positive was the experience I gained—but it came at a very high price.

Meanwhile, HSIL continued to go from strength to strength. It has earned a profit every year, missed paying dividends only once in the more than fifty years of its existence and has a strong balance sheet. This has been possible only because of close supervision, constant innovation, investment in the best technology and strong systems.

Several new players entered the market in the 1980s in the wake of our success. Many thought, from our example, that it was easy to make money and all they had to do was hit the market with competing products. But reality proved very different. None of the five or six companies that came up in that period made any money. Some ran for six months, some for twelve and one for two years before shutting shop.

Parry bought two of these companies, I bought two. The rest shut down.

I recalled Twyfords chairman Jack Hay's prophetic words. 'In the sanitaryware industry, profits depend on supervision.' Once again, I was thankful for his guidance and training early in my career.

HSIL had, over the years, become a national brand. But servicing the south Indian market was proving to be challenging. Freight costs were high, impacting margins. Then, our production in Haryana was sold out. Two decades after starting out, we were still struggling to keep pace with demand.

I bought a plot of land near Hyderabad to set up another sanitaryware plant to service the south Indian market. Around this time, Krishna Ceramics, a small sanitaryware company, came up for sale. Its promoter, one Mr Yashashwi, was one of the entrepreneurs who had entered the industry seeing our success and our margin of 30 per cent. He couldn't earn a paisa from his venture and after a couple of years, decided to cut his losses and exit. His plant was small, churning out about 5,00,000 units of sanitaryware every year. I bought it for ₹72 lakh through an exchange of shares.

This meant I no longer needed another plant in the south. I sold the plot I had bought and focused my attention on expanding the unit I had bought. Over the years, this plant has prospered and is doing very well, allowing HSIL to comfortably service the entire south Indian market.

By the 2000s, HSIL had weathered the storm unleashed in the Indian market by economic reforms and the entry of several foreign brands and emerged stronger. Despite the increased competition, both from foreign rivals as well as from cheap Chinese imports, on which there were no countervailing duties, HSIL has retained its numero uno position in the Indian market.

BRINGING THE RAINBOW

Though we have managed to go from strength to strength, the market has actually become a lot more difficult. We have been able to cope only because of the strong systems I have built over the years. Not only has competition become cut-throat, the quality of the trade and of the people involved in it has also deteriorated.

Cheques issued by debtors bounce much more often than they did earlier, despite strict laws and numerous court orders clamping down on the practice. I cannot understand how anyone can issue a cheque when he knows his bank balance does not justify it. It isn't as if cheques didn't bounce earlier. But there was shame and social stigma attached to it. Now, people just brazen it out. This reeks of the reckless business culture that some people have adopted. Perhaps it is also linked to the new get-rich-fast-at-any-cost philosophy that seems to be guiding some of the younger people today.

Things have gotten worse since the slowdown began in 2011. Sanitaryware is always the last item that realtors buy. With the real-estate sector stagnant at best and contracting at worst, I expect things to get worse before they get better. Realtors will have to start discounting to sell their housing stock. But with these companies having earned supernormal profits in the preceding decade, they probably have the wherewithal to hold their prices, even if sales don't pick up, for a little while longer.

Chinese imports are a major source of irritation. They are mostly of questionable quality, but being cheap, appeal to some customers. The duty structure works against domestic manufacturers, but I guess Indian industry has to live with it.

I faced another peculiar problem with China. I was shocked when my president informed me in 2014 that our brand, Hindware, was already registered in China by a local company and hence our application to register the brand had been rejected.

We moved court to restrain the Chinese company from using our brand but our plea was rejected by the Chinese courts. We then began negotiations, through our lawyer, with the company that had registered Hindware in its name, to sell the brand back to us. The negotiations continued for a while, with neither side willing to bend, but I finally managed to 'buy' back my brand at a high price. It was only then that I could register Hindware in China.

This was an unprecedented situation. I had read about cyber squatters registering the trade names of big companies on the Internet and then selling it back to the rightful owners for large sums of money, but couldn't believe that I was facing a situation that was worse.

It meant that any future plans of exporting my products to China and, conceivably, other markets around the world, were in jeopardy.

It was a wake-up call. After consulting experts, I decided not to take any more chances and registered my brand name in various markets across the world. It cost HSIL a packet but it provided insurance against a repetition of this incident in future.

Sandip's coming of age and assumption of greater responsibilities left me with more time to focus on other areas. HSIL's had a strong balance sheet and comfortable cash reserves. It was the market leader in sanitaryware and enjoyed a strong position in the glass-bottles industry. I began to look at opportunities for expansion in related sectors.

In 2008, I bought a factory in the United Kingdom that makes products for differently abled people. A year later, HSIL set up a new glass plant in Bhongir in Andhra Pradesh (now Telangana) with a melting capacity of 950 tonnes a day at a cost of ₹700 crore.

AGI, which I had bought in 1981, is now profitable and makes

BRINGING THE RAINBOW

the distinctly shaped Quink ink bottles as well as bottles for several popular whisky and beer brands. In 2015, at an investment of ₹80 crore, I set up a division called AGI Clozures to make special security caps for whisky bottles. I also bought Garden Polymers Pvt Ltd, which has two plants, one in Dharwad in Karnataka and another in Selaqui in Uttarakhand, making PET bottles and caps for Royal Stag and Bagpiper whisky brands and several others.

I began thinking once again of getting into the bathroom-fittings segment. Because of the high brand recall of Hindware, it made sense to get into this segment. People were actively seeking our sanitaryware products. We enjoyed tremendous goodwill with dealers and customers alike. And in most cases, the same dealers who sold wash basins, water closets, etc., also sold taps, faucets and shower heads. So, we had a ready-made channel to reach the customer. All we needed was a set of quality products that lived up to the trust that our sanitaryware products enjoyed.

Although we had got our fingers badly burnt with Soma Plumbing, I had learnt my lessons. Determined not to repeat them, in 2010, I bought a plant manufacturing bathroom fittings in Bhiwadi from Havells for ₹18 crore. A new greenfield plant making chrome-plated taps and other bathroom fittings went into production last year in Kehrani in Rajasthan. These products are marketed under the Hindware and Benelave brands.

We have also launched a brand of electric geysers under the Hindware Atlantic brand. These are early days and we are currently buying these geysers from a French vendor. Hopefully, the volumes will pick up sufficiently to justify the setting up or acquisition of a plant to manufacture these in-house.

Thus, HSIL has emerged as a one-stop shop for all bathroom solutions.

All these expansions have been funded by internal accruals and loans. It is a matter of pride that all my eight factories are running well and all of them are earning profits. This wouldn't have been possible without the hard work and active cooperation of all my colleagues, workers and external stakeholders. I take this opportunity to thank each one of them for making HSIL what it is today.

Competition in the market has now become even more intense following the entry of many more global brands. HSIL competes with them at the top end of the market, where some of the products are very high tech and extremely high priced. The buyers are usually businessmen and leading executives and professionals who are well travelled and exposed to the latest products in developed countries. They carefully research competing brands and often visit several showrooms before making a final selection.

To create a buzz about the Hindware Italian Collection, Hindware Art and Hindware, our three sub-brands that cater to different segments of the market, we decided to rope in Bollywood superstar and youth icon Shah Rukh Khan, aka SRK (as millions of his fans call him), as the brand ambassador.

This was Sandip's initiative and he handled all the details of the negotiations and finalization of the agreement. The advertising campaign cost HSIL a pretty packet, but it is worth every hard-earned paisa. The day we announced the association between HSIL and SRK, he released the following statement: '*Brand Hindware has been synonymous with bathroom products for many years and has truly captured the shift in perception in this space. The awareness that they have is visible in their products, offering contemporary design solutions for bathrooms. It is the brand's steadfast approach and revolutionary intent that makes Hindware an exciting brand and I am looking forward to our association.*'

Though I did not personally interact much with SRK, Sandip and other senior executives who worked closely with him were left scratching their heads in awe.

He shot for the ad film and posed for campaign photographs till the wee hours of the morning with an energy and verve that left everyone spellbound. Then, as he wasn't happy with some of the sequences, he gave us additional dates, free of cost, to reshoot those sequences to ensure that the ad was at par with the best.

I also discovered that he is a thorough professional who takes an interest in every aspect of the campaigns he is involved with. Every branding featuring his image has to be sent to him for clearance. He personally chooses every photograph of his that the campaign can use.

When my son and a few senior executives recounted the story of the re-shoot to me, I appreciated SRK's professionalism, his attention to detail and his fierce loyalty to his own brand. These are rare qualities that deserve admiration. I realized then why he has emerged heads and shoulders above his peers to be regarded as the Badshah of Bollywood.

The ad campaign has created a new buzz about the Hindware brand and raised its profile. This campaign is our most high-profile tryst with Bollywood, but it isn't the first or only one. In the movie *Shamitabh*, superstar Amitabh Bachchan is shown sitting on a Hindware commode. We have also signed on Bollywood actress Jacqueline Fernandez for our brand Queo, which is registered in England.

The only part of my business that isn't doing well is Evok, a fully owned subsidiary of HSIL, which runs a chain of large-format furniture and home-decor stores. However, I am optimistic that the situation will improve as the Indian economy claws its way back to a higher growth trajectory.

In retrospect, I am really grateful to my family for its decision to move me out of Calcutta more than half a century ago. I wouldn't have become who I am had I remained there.

10

FAMILY FEUD AND PARTITION

By the mid-1970s, the Somany family had established itself in industry and was counted among the leading business houses in the country. We had successfully established HNG, HSIL and Somany Pilkington, each a leader in its segment, had a partnership with S.R. Damani in Simplex Mills and had also bought Soma Textiles through a court auction.

Each of us six brothers—Bhaiji, Onkar Bhaiji, Surendra Kumar, Chandra Kumar, Lalit and I—held an equal one-sixth share in the business. Each of us, however, had clearly demarcated responsibilities. Onkar Bhaiji and Chandra Kumar ran HNG, Surendra Kumar looked after our interests in Simplex and ran Soma Textiles with Lalit, and I was in charge of HSIL. Bhaiji, who was looking after Somany Pilkington, was also chairman of HSIL.

To the outside world, we were a phalanx. Though we lived in

different cities—Surendra Kumar in Bombay, Lalit in Ahmedabad, I in Delhi and the rest of my brothers in Calcutta—we met regularly every year and on social occasions. We stayed at each other's houses when visiting the four cities and kept everyone informed about the businesses in our charge. But strains had begun to surface in this 'united and happy family' image we portrayed to the outside world—and their roots lay in the past.

My maternal uncle, Ratan Mamaji, had visited me in England in 1961 and spent a night at my flat. He gave me a ten-page handwritten letter from Lalit in which my youngest brother made grave and damaging allegations against Onkar Bhaiji. Purely by chance, he said, he had happened to check the share transfer register of HNG, our first successful industrial venture, and had discovered evidence of manipulation of the ownership structure. This, he alleged, was being done by Onkar Bhaiji.

I was stunned and wanted to show Bhaiji the letter, but Ratan Mamaji refused to hand it over. 'I only wanted to show you the letter to warn you,' he said. I duly wrote to Bhaiji about Lalit's warning. I'm not sure what transpired between my two oldest brothers, but a strain began to appear between Onkar Bhaiji and the rest of us.

This simmering tension reared its ugly head in the 1970s, sparking off a major crisis in the family and the business and resulting in the arrest of two of my executives and a threat to have me arrested if I stepped into Haryana, where my Bahadurgarh factory is located.

The genesis of this crisis dated back to the time when we were setting up a glass plant in Rishra, West Bengal, under Hindusthan National Glass Manufacturing Company Ltd, which was renamed Hindusthan National Glass Ltd (HNG) in 1971.

As I have mentioned earlier, Bhaiji had previously made

two unsuccessful attempts at entering the manufacturing sector. Encouraged by Onkar Bhaiji's father-in-law B.M. Birla, we embarked on this venture.

The project was estimated to cost ₹20 lakh. IFCI, a leading financial institution, agreed to provide 50 per cent of the project cost as a loan. That meant we had to raise the remaining ₹10 lakh. The company had equity capital of ₹5 lakh and preference capital of ₹5 lakh. The Bangur family, with whom Bhaiji had excellent relations, agreed to subscribe to the entire preference capital.

At that time, we were in a position to invest only ₹2 lakh, leaving a gaping deficit of ₹3 lakh in the company's equity base. Bhaiji approached B.M. Birla, who agreed to subscribe to the company's equity and invest ₹3 lakh. That, however, meant that B.M. Birla, with a 60 per cent stake, was the effective owner of the company, while we, the official promoters, held a minority 40 per cent stake.

Unfortunately, there was a cost overrun of ₹8 lakh, which threw all our calculations out of gear. IFCI insisted that we put up half that amount, ₹4 lakh, as additional equity. That was a massive sum of money in those days. We didn't have any more funds to invest. So, Onkar Bhaiji requested his father-in-law to pitch in. B.M. Birla refused to invest any further.

Bhaiji and Onkar Bhaiji were very dejected and it seemed for a while that our third attempt at making the transition from trade to industry would meet the same fate as the previous two. But Bhaiji was not one to remain down for long. Always a fighter and with his never-say-die attitude, he approached his father-in-law, Shah Goverdhanlalji Kabra, and convinced him to pitch in with ₹4 lakh. Thus, the project was back on track.

Subsequently, Kabraji gifted his shares to Kamla Bhabi, his daughter, who magnanimously gifted them equally to all six of us.

This meant that the Somany family's share in the increased capital base of ₹9 lakh increased to 66.67 per cent while the Birla share fell to 33.33 per cent.

We were now owners of the company.

But unknown to us, Onkar Bhaiji was planning to wrest control of HNG. Soon after the company became profitable, B.M. Birla transferred his shares to his daughter, Ganga Bhabi. It was these transfers that Lalit had stumbled upon and written to me about while I was training with Twyfords. Taken together with Onkar Bhaiji's 11.11 per cent stake, he and his wife owned 44.44 per cent of the company. If Onkar Bhaiji could buy out the stake of any of the other five brothers, he would gain majority and sole control of the company to the exclusion of the rest of us. He was already chairman of HNG, having made it clear from the beginning that he would settle for nothing less. Bhaiji had agreed to this probably because of the active help, guidance and financial support being provided by the Birlas.

The company's equity base, meanwhile, had increased to almost ₹70 lakh following a number of bonus issues, but the shareholding pattern remained more or less the same.

Late one afternoon, Ganga Bhabi dropped in at my house in Vasant Vihar. While tea was being served, she deeply appreciated my collection of various brands of pottery, which I had bought during my stay in England in 1961. Because of my liking for pottery, I had kept adding to my collection.

Just as she was leaving, she said I could add to my collection any of the best pottery that was available. I felt this was a precursor to an offer to buy out my shares in HNG.

She read my body language correctly and left shortly thereafter. I learnt later that Onkar Bhaiji had sent Surendra Kumar, Chandra

Kumar and Lalit similar feelers, but all of them had refused to part with their shares.

To the best of my recollections, by 1971, relations between Onkar Bhaiji and the rest of us had deteriorated to the point where we were barely on speaking terms. There was the very real apprehension that Onkar Bhaiji might yet, with the backing of the Birlas, manage to buy out one of the brothers and gain full control of HNG, leaving the rest of us out in the cold.

We needed a strategy to ring-fence ourselves against any such attempt. At Surendra Kumar's suggestion, we decided to set up two holding companies, New Delhi Industrial Promoters & Investors Ltd (NDIPIL) and Soma Investments Ltd. Each of us five brothers transferred 6.6 per cent of our individual stakes in HNG to these companies, leaving only 4.4 per cent in each of our individual names. In return, each of us received a 20 per cent stake in the two holding companies. Thus, even if Onkar Bhaiji did manage to win over one brother, he would at best get a 48.8 per cent stake in the company. To get a majority, he would need to buy out the individual stakes of at least two brothers, which would be extremely difficult.

This idea of ring-fencing our interests in HNG came just in time. My youngest brother Lalit, who had first discovered Onkar Bhaiji's efforts to gain a majority in HNG and had warned me about it, passed away the following year, on 22 February 1972, at the young age of thirty-two.

Following this, Onkar Bhaiji, with the backing of the Birlas, managed to win over Lalit's widow Sunita. She left Somany House, which my brothers had built at 2 Iron Side Road in Calcutta, and also filed several legal cases against Bhaiji, Surendra Kumar, Chandra Kumar and me, on behalf of her minor son Rajat and herself, for the cancellation of various share transfers that had been done for tax-saving purposes. The intent was clear: Onkar Bhaiji was firing from her shoulder to get the incremental 1.2 per cent stake he needed to gain majority control of HNG.

We were in a quandary. The Birlas were the biggest and most powerful business family in the country. They had helped us on numerous occasions. We were also related to them through two marriages. Apart from Onkar Bhaiji being B.M. Birla's son-in-law, the venerable G.D. Birla's first wife, L.N. Birla's mother, had been our aunt. In his childhood and early youth, L.N. Birla had spent many a summer holiday at our house on Ratu Sarkar Lane. And Bhaiji continued to enjoy excellent relations with the Birlas.

Taking on the might of the Birla clan and engaging in a proxy battle for control of a company wasn't something we were spoiling for. But HNG was our crown jewel and we couldn't just let it slip out of our control.

We decided to fight Onkar Bhaiji and Sunita in court and were vindicated when the Supreme Court ruled in our favour in 1978–1979. Though Onkar Bhaiji continued to run the company as chairman, the remaining four brothers remained majority shareholders with a 51.2 per cent stake.

All this while, Chandra Kumar had continued to work in HNG, despite his (and our) differences with Onkar Bhaiji. HNG and HSIL shared the same factory premises in Bahadurgarh, where I worked, but I was too involved with my own affairs at HSIL and with the various public institutions that I was associated with to pay too much attention to the battle that had broken out within the family. I was kept informed of all that was going on and fully supported the stand of Bhaijji and the others against Onkar Bhaiji, but scrupulously avoided personal involvement in the family dispute.

BRINGING THE RAINBOW

It must have been a difficult situation for Chandra Kumar. He had come out openly on our side of the family but was working in a company of which Onkar Bhaiji was chairman. I do not know how the two of them managed to run the affairs of HNG despite pulling so obviously in opposite directions.

It has struck me in retrospect, three decades after the dispute was finally settled following Onkar Bhaiji's demise in 1985, that the four of us had a majority in HNG and were, therefore, in a position to remove Onkar Bhaiji from the management of the company. I do not know why we didn't. All I know is that it never came up for discussion. I can only surmise that Bhaiji and Chandra Kumar, who were on the frontlines of the fight, perhaps did not want to antagonize the Birlas any further. But I hasten to add that this is just conjecture on my part. I have never asked my brothers about this and none of them have ever told me the reason for their reluctance to decisively defeat Onkar Bhaiji.

My relations with Onkar Bhaiji reached their nadir during the mid-1970s. Emergency had just been declared. Bansi Lal was the chief minister of Haryana, where the HNG and HSIL factories were located. As many will remember, those were the darkest days for democracy in India. Civil rights were suspended. Political leaders, activists, journalists and thousands of others were rounded up and jailed without legal recourse. Citizens were picked up by the police on mere suspicion. There were several cases of politicians and influential people settling personal scores by getting rivals arrested. The draconian Maintenance of Internal Security Act (MISA) was used to intimidate businessmen and traders suspected not only of indulging in black marketeering and other corrupt practices but also of funding opposition parties. An ominous cloak of fear and dread hung like a shroud over boardrooms across the country.

My family, and I in particular, had always steered clear of politics. The sanitaryware business, which I handled on behalf of my family, did not require me to interact with government departments on a regular basis except for the purpose of paying taxes and some compliance issues. My products could not, under any circumstances, be deemed to be 'essential' goods. I had also taken pains to ensure that HSIL and its dealers did not generate any black money by selling my products at an illegal premium. And finally, I had put in place systems to ensure that all statutory dues owed by HSIL were paid well before the due date, going to the extent of penalizing executives who waited till the last day to remit taxes and other dues.

Therefore, it came as a shock when the sales tax department of the Government of Haryana raided my plant in March 1975 and seized all my books of accounts without any explanation. Regular enquiries about the fate of the books and any related investigations met with no response. A couple of months passed. The last date for presenting my annual accounts was drawing close. Failure to do so would result in stringent punishment. But my auditors couldn't even start the process of auditing my books, which were in the custody of the state.

I decided to approach the courts for relief. My well-wishers were shocked and advised me against such 'legal and political adventurism'. 'You can't pick a fight with the crocodile if you wish to survive in the water,' they warned, quoting a popular Hindi saying.

It was a Catch-22 situation. I risked political retribution if I dragged the state government to court. But I also risked stringent and punitive action against the directors of the company, which included Bhaiji, who was chairman of the HSIL board, and myself, if I failed to present audited accounts for the previous financial year within the stipulated time.

It was quite obvious to me why I had been raided. I also knew whose invisible hand was pulling the strings from behind the scenes. Perhaps the intention was precisely to place me in this situation: where I would be damned if I did and damned if I didn't.

Once again, I was faced with a matter of principle and I was damned if I was going to compromise. I told my well-wishers that I would move heaven and earth to comply with my statutory responsibilities, which was to file the audited accounts of HSIL before the authorities by the due date, even if it meant rubbing the powers that be the wrong way. I moved court to have my books released from the sales tax department.

I was vindicated when the high court ruled in my favour. The sales tax department was forced to return my books. It was perilously close to the deadline, but I was determined not to default. Working day and night, pushing my team beyond all reasonable limits, I managed to complete the audit and presented my accounts to the authorities and my shareholders within the statutory deadline.

I had won round one against my invisible adversary quite decisively. But the enemy was resourceful, politically well connected and determined. We braced for round two, which we were sure would be more vicious and severe.

The expected political backlash wasn't too long in coming. On 19 November that year, two senior executives of HSIL and two of Bhaiji's senior executives from Somany Pilkington, which he managed, were arrested under the dreaded MISA law. As was the case with the sales tax raid, the Haryana authorities gave no explanation regarding the nature of the charges against them. This was yet another attempt to browbeat us into submission.

Interestingly, no one from HNG, which had its factory in the same plot as HSIL, was touched.

The executives were released after about three weeks on 11 December, again without any explanation.

With this ploy also failing, my adversary was getting desperate. I was informed by some people that I would be arrested if I entered Haryana. This meant I couldn't visit my factory to supervise its operations as I was wont to do. The idea seemed to be to cripple the functioning of HSIL and harass Somany Pilkington in order to bring us down to our knees and then force us to sell out on the cheap.

I couldn't visit my factory for more than two months. Work suffered, but fortunately, the systems I had put in place proved robust enough to withstand these disruptions and see us through those difficult times. I fled to Ahmedabad as there was the very real fear that the Haryana authorities would try to arrest me in Delhi. In Ahmedabad, I didn't stay with my relatives but with a third party. This was a very difficult phase in my life. I was dealing with the sudden and mysterious deaths of my first and second wives, struggling to bring up three young children as well as trying to stay afloat in the political, administrative and personal storms that were buffeting my life from all sides. But my family and I survived and lived to tell the tale, thanks to the grace of God and the good wishes of my friends and associates.

Emergency was finally lifted on 21 March 1977, as suddenly as it had been imposed. The dark clouds that had hung over the entire country—including my family, our companies and our executives—lifted and life slowly returned to normal.

Onkar Bhaiji passed away in London in October 1985. He had been a regular morning walker, took his medicines and ate a very restricted diet. Though I hadn't been in touch with him, I was shocked at the news, which I received while I was at a Rotary Club meeting.

Death is a great leveller. Despite our differences and our often acrimonious fight for the control of HNG, we decided to go to London for his last rites. But there were no return flights available till almost a fortnight after the funeral. Surendra Kumar, Chandra Kumar and I had pressing engagements and couldn't afford to stay in London for such a long time. Finally, only Bhaiji and Kamla Bhabi made the trip to London and represented the family at Onkar Bhaiji's funeral.

Soon after that, we came to a settlement with Onkar Bhaiji's sons, Shashi and Vikram, and also with Sunita, Lalit's widow, under which we acquired their shares in HNG and all other group companies. Thus, by the mid-1980s, four of us—Bhaiji, Surendra Kumar, Chandra Kumar and I—became the joint owners of 100 per cent of the Somany holdings in our group companies.

Onkar Bhaiji had purchased Madhusudan Industries, a leading maker of ghee, some years prior to his death. His sons took over the reins of the company following his death and also floated Cera Ceramics, which makes sanitaryware.

A few years later, Shashi, who is a chemical engineer from MIT and the first Somany to study abroad, exited the business and settled down in London. Onkar Bhaiji's younger son Vikram now runs Madhusudan Industries and Cera Ceramics, both of which, I'm happy to say, are doing well. Cera, which is about a third the size of HSIL, competes with me in the market. Between HSIL and Cera, we command an overwhelming 55 per cent share of the Indian sanitaryware market.

The rest of the decade passed without any major development. Our businesses—HNG, now managed on behalf of the family by Chandra Kumar, HSIL and Somany Pilkington—grew steadily. Soma Textiles, run by Surendra Kumar, however, suffered as a result of the headwinds faced by the textiles industry.

My son Sandip joined the business in 1989 and the decade, which had opened with so much turmoil within the family, ended on a peaceful note.

The 1990s brought the financial crisis of 1991, when decades of flawed economic policies, mandated by the ideology that successive governments had followed, came back to haunt the country. The economy nosedived and our foreign exchange reserves plummeted to a level where they were just enough to cover three weeks of imports. There was the very real fear of the country defaulting on its international financial obligations. The minority government of P.V. Narasimha Rao, which came to power following the tragic assassination of Rajiv Gandhi, appointed economist and former Reserve Bank of India governor Manmohan Singh as finance minister. Singh set about repairing the damage caused by his predecessors by opening up the economy, cutting red tape and pulling back the government's overbearing presence in every sphere of economic decision-making.

The 1990s were an interesting time for the Somany family as well. Bhaiji's grandson Abhishek returned to India after completing his higher studies in the United Kingdom and joined the business in the early 1990s, the first member of the third generation of the Somany clan to do so. He was armed with the latest management thinking and trained to do things very differently from the way we had been running our companies. Other next-generation Somany family members were waiting in the wings—pursuing higher studies abroad—to take the group forward.

There was still complete understanding among the four

remaining founders of the group and our children also got along very well. But I foresaw possible problems that could arise from the entry of our grandchildren into the business, with their different thinking. I wasn't certain that the familial ties and the strict Marwari culture that had kept us brothers closely bonded through our lives would endure into the third generation and beyond, and felt that maybe the time had come to divide our businesses and other assets amicably among us.

I had seen far too many instances of families avoiding taking this step while the going was good only to regret it later when disagreements and conflicts among younger family members and their spouses had erupted into full-scale court battles that had destroyed much of what earlier generations had created. In many such instances, members of older generations, who had lived in harmony all their lives, had got involved on the side of their progeny, damaging and even breaking the bonds that had bound them till then, thus completely destroying the goodwill that they had jointly spent their lives building. I was adamant that my extended family should not meet with the same fate.

I broached the topic somewhat gingerly with my brothers, uncertain of the reception my idea would receive. Fortunately, they welcomed the idea and we got down to the difficult and delicate task of carving up the pie.

We had four main operating companies, each managed by one brother, but owned jointly and equally by all four. Unlike other business families, we had not invested much in real estate, paintings, antiques, and other assets. Each brother owned a house, but these had been bought from our personal resources, and therefore belonged to each individual. So there were no parallel streams of income flowing into our privately held companies. We reinvested most of the money we earned from our operating companies back into our businesses and this had allowed us to consolidate our position in the marketplace.

This had created a unique problem for me in particular. Since dividends from our companies went mostly to our jointly owned holding companies, each brother had a claim over these resources when we needed money for expansion or acquisitions. Being the youngest of the four surviving brothers, my claims were often overridden by the others in favour of their own plans for the companies they ran. It may surprise many readers that this was so, but this is the way Indian business families operate. Resisting it or protesting too vehemently against such 'discrimination'—there is no other word to describe it—would have meant breaking the unspoken family code and could have led to a parting of ways with my brothers. Deeply ingrained cultural values and strong family bonds prevented me—and indeed, all my remaining brothers—from going down this road when the family consensus worked against any one of us. 'Great deeds are achieved by great sacrifices only,' Swami Vivekananda had said. As far as we were concerned, a small curtailment in our operating freedom was a small price to pay for the benefits of remaining united.

We had to first discuss the methodology for the family partition. I suggested that we should put down our agreement in writing so that there would be no misunderstandings later. My apprehensions proved well-founded, as the family went through a second round of convulsions by the time we finished carving up the businesses among ourselves.

Let me explain why I wanted our agreement set in stone. We were in the process of dividing assets worth hundreds, perhaps thousands, of crores. Power and wealth within the family was asymmetrically divided. Those who controlled more profitable companies were naturally in a stronger position than those whose companies weren't doing as well. Besides, it wasn't just a deal between four brothers. Our children, grandchildren and spouses would also obviously have an important, though not decisive, say in the final outcome. Though none of them owned a large enough chunk of shares to make a difference, individual brothers, now considering their own and the future of their families as standalone business groups, would obviously seek inputs from their respective families. I wanted us to avoid a situation where afterthoughts and late realizations could throw a carefully considered separation plan into question.

Opposition came from a source I had least anticipated. Bhaiji, who was, by consensus, the head of the family, suddenly flew into a rage at one of our meetings. He got up from his chair and shouted: 'You don't trust me? I'm not going to sign anything. If we wish to continue, we can discuss, debate and finalize our understanding, but no agreement will be signed.' Even though I was approaching sixty, respect for Bhaiji stopped me from protesting against what I felt was a rigid and impractical stand. My son Sandip was also strongly in favour of a written agreement, but that was not to be.

Each brother owned a 25 per cent stake in the combined businesses of the family. But given the different sizes, profitability and asset bases of various group companies, each brother did not control a proportionate share of the family assets. We needed a scientific valuation of all assets we owned before they could be divided. Accordingly, we engaged Pricewaterhouse Coopers (PwC), a Big 4 consulting firm, to conduct a group-wide valuation exercise and suggest the most efficient way of dividing the business.

After a few months, and following some suggestions from us,

it devised a valuation and partition formula that was acceptable to all of us. According to this, each of us brothers could opt to retain control of one of our four main operating companies by buying out the shares of the remaining three brothers. But if a brother wanted a company that was under the management of another, he would have to pay a premium over the agreed price.

I was certain from the beginning that I wanted to keep HSIL. I had been with the company from day one and had built it from scratch. Except for the warehouse, I had bought every brick that went into the company and had also recruited every senior executive who worked for it. I had no doubt received unstinting support from Bhaiji, Surendra Kumar and Chandra Kumar, but I could honestly claim the credit for nurturing HSIL from birth to the market leader that it had become. I knew nothing of the textiles sector, and so had no interest in Soma Textiles or in any of the other group companies. Fortunately, my brothers also felt the same way and it was decided that each of us would retain the company we controlled and buy out the stakes of the remaining brothers in it at a pre-agreed valuation.

Sometime before we finalized the family partition, Nalini Bhabi, Surendra Kumar's wife, compelled him to give some shares to our sisters, Sushilabai and Sarlabai. 'They are your sisters, so they should also benefit from the family's success and join in the happiness,' she said. It was a very magnanimous gesture on her part. It takes a large heart and utter selflessness to give away shares worth crores of rupees—a king's ransom even today and worth a lot more in relative terms two decades ago—and kudos to Nalini Bhabi for having the courage to do so even though there was no compulsion.

Sushilabai was given shares in the names of her daughters, Jayshree and Sunanda. These were purchased by Chandra Kumar.

He also purchased the shares given to Sarlabai. Following these internal family settlements, Chandra Kumar became owner of 40 per cent of HNG shares while Bhaiji, Surendra Kumar and I were left with a 20 per cent stake each in the company.

In 1995, several months after our verbal agreement to separate amicably, Chandra Kumar offered to buy HNG shares from the remaining three brothers at ₹267 per share as had been agreed on 5 August 1995. I did not participate in this offer as I had no immediate need for additional funds but Bhaiji and Surendra Kumar sold a portion of their stakes, thus, raising Chandra Kumar's shareholding in HNG to a little more than 51 per cent. HNG also came out with a large rights issue. Bhaiji, Surendra Kumar and I renounced our rights in favour of Chandra Kumar. This took his stake up to almost 60 per cent.

At this point, a dispute arose over the interpretation of the verbal family agreement. Based on our understanding of that pact, Bhaiji, Surendra Kumar and I demanded a particular price. But Chandra Kumar had a different interpretation of that agreement and refused. We waited for two years. Several informal parleys were held, but we failed to make any headway towards a settlement that we considered fair. Finally, in 1997, Bhaiji, Surendra Kumar and I filed a case against Chandra Kumar in the Calcutta High Court to force him to buy our stakes in HNG at the agreed price plus interest.

Meanwhile, the textiles sector, once the source of so many great Indian fortunes, was experiencing a downturn. In line with industry trends, Soma Textiles also suffered. Sometime during the pendency of our suit in the Calcutta High Court, Surendra Kumar sold his shares to Chandra Kumar at a price much lower than the agreed ₹267 per share plus interest.

R.K. SOMANY

The high court ruled in Chandra Kumar's favour. The verdict was upheld in appeal all the way to the Supreme Court. Chandra Kumar now made an offer to buy us out at ₹64.17 per share plus interest of ₹17.11 per share as per Sebi guidelines, against our estimate, based on our understanding of the verbal agreement we had reached in 1995, of about ₹700 per share, inclusive of interest.

Though I didn't point it out, my fears about Bhaiji's refusal to put down our mutual partition terms in writing had been borne out by unfolding events.

According to calculations based on the formula we had agreed upon at the time of partition, I was supposed to receive ₹32.76 crore plus interest. Instead, I received only ₹4.90 crore.

A dispute also erupted between Bhaiji and Surendra Kumar, but I am unaware of the details. I enjoy excellent relations with both and so have steered clear of attempts made by mutual friends to get me to play arbitrator between them.

Unfortunately, I can't say the same about the state of my ties with Chandra Kumar. In my view, he reneged on a verbal family agreement. I understand that he feels the same way about me for reasons I haven't been able to fathom, but I'm sure he has his reasons. As the old English saying goes: The wearer knows where the shoe pinches. I haven't met or spoken to Chandra Kumar in more than a decade.

While parting ways, we brothers decided that we had to do something for our nephew M.K. Daga, my eldest sister's son, who had spent most of his life working with us. He had also made crucial contributions to our success at critical times, and it would be unfair and indeed, unethical, to leave him high and dry as we divided the family pie among us. We had taken great care and maybe even sacrificed the possibility of growing further because of our determination to be fair.

In 1994, when we agreed on the partition, he was managing Somany Pilkington and Orient Ceramics, a company we had taken over from its erstwhile promoters, under the overall supervision of Bhaiji. With the concurrence of all the brothers, we decided to transfer the ownership and control of Orient Ceramics to M.K. Daga, though we had no legal obligation to do so. The company has grown under his stewardship to a turnover of about ₹300 crore.

Bhaiji is now ninety-six, my brothers Surendra Kumar and Chandra Kumar are both in their eighties and I am seventy-eight. Except for Bhaiji, who has retired from all businesses, the rest of us remain actively involved with our companies.

Bhaiji's company, Somany Ceramics (earlier called Somany Pikington), a major player, in floor tiles, is now managed by his son Shreekant. Both of them live in Delhi and we remain in regular touch. Surendra Kumar lives in Mumbai and manages Soma Textiles with his son Arvind. The company is not doing well and this is a cause of concern for the entire family.

Chandra Kumar and his two sons, Sanjay and Mukul, run the affairs of HNG. As I have said earlier, I have little contact with them.

Onkar Bhaiji's sons are also doing well. After turning cold for the duration of my dispute with her husband, my relations with Ganga Bhabi have once again regained the warmth that had marked them in my early years. I speak to her at least twice or thrice every month and make it a point to look her—and my sisters Sushilabai and Sarlabai—up every time I visit Calcutta.

11

ECONOMIC LIBERALIZATION OF 1991: NEW CHALLENGES, NEW OPPORTUNITIES

Prior to 1991, India had a bizarre law called the Monopolies and Restrictive Trade Practices Act, which deemed any company or group with an annual turnover of ₹100 crore or more to be a 'monopoly house' whose activities had to be controlled and whose growth had to be stunted.

A country grappling with chronic shortages of almost everything and debilitating levels of unemployment also actually had another law that penalized companies for producing more than their rated capacities. The penalty for the managements of such companies could range from hefty fines to, believe it or not, a jail term.

The political elite had propounded the preposterous theory since Independence that such laws benefitted the poor by preventing the so-called concentration of wealth in the hands of a few. Four-and-a half decades after 1947, there was no evidence of socialism uplifting the lot of the poor, but it definitely helped the socialists, or at least those who claimed to follow socialism, maintain a vice-like grip over power. Corruption was rampant, shortages chronic and the quality of all products shoddy.

For millions of people, the only route out of grinding poverty was the benevolence and munificence of politicians and their clients in the business world. Only members of a tightly controlled club of politicians, businessmen and wheeler-dealers had the wherewithal to dole out favours in the forms of jobs or contracts. This perpetuated a cycle of crony capitalism, all-round poverty and widespread disillusionment.

Today, two-thirds of Indians are below the age of thirty. Such readers will find it difficult to believe the conditions that existed before the economic liberalization of the nineties, but a couple of examples will perhaps help them understand. It took years to get a simple telephone connection—and that too only if one had a recommendation from a member of Parliament, a member of the legislative assembly or other senior government official. Then, such connections would remain out of order for months together even as the state-owned monopoly in charge of telecommunications continued to send exorbitant bills. Any complaints would be met with a stock reply: 'cable fault'.

We even had to live through times when the government, in its wisdom, raised the income tax level to 97 per cent—again to allegedly prevent concentration of wealth in the hands of a few. Naturally, leakages, tax evasion and bribery to keep taxmen away became the order of the day. Tax collections suffered and the country slowly ground its way to bankruptcy.

That finally happened in 1990–91. Decades of socialism finally came home to roost when India's foreign-exchange reserves dipped to such a precarious level that they were enough to cover only three weeks of imports. India was forced to pledge 20 tonnes of gold to the Bank of England to stave off a default, setting the stage for far-reaching reforms that are still a work in progress.

Economic liberalization was ushered in by an unlikely duo—Prime Minister P.V. Narasimha Rao, who came out of retirement to head the government following the tragic assassination of former prime minister Rajiv Gandhi, and finance minister Manmohan Singh, a highly respected economist who had previously served as the governor of the Reserve Bank of India and also as secretary in the finance ministry, among other important bureaucratic assignments.

It was ironic. The two main architects of economic reforms had been important pillars of the political establishment that had scripted and followed policies that had brought India to its knees. Now, they were in charge of an administration that took upon itself the mandate of pulling down the very edifice that they had, directly or indirectly, helped erect and replacing it with a system that respected merit and efficiency.

Indian industry, long shackled by unreasonable restrictions and a rent-seeking administration, by and large welcomed the change in economic philosophy, but it soon became evident that it wasn't prepared for it. There were very real fears of Indian businesses being overwhelmed and rolled over by foreign competition and cheap imports.

In my opinion, it would have been better if the government had given us a two-year window to prepare for an open economy. Instead, it was like a bedridden patient being forced to compete with world-class athletes without being given a chance at convalescence.

That Indian industry adjusted well to the new circumstances

and the country's economy went from strength to strength, raising growth rates and lifting millions from poverty, speaks volumes about the resilience of the country's psyche and the strength of its human capital.

But the process has been a difficult one. New environments inevitably throw up new sets of winners and also-rans. If one looks back, many of the top business groups, or 'monopoly houses' as they were called then, no longer feature among the leading conglomerates in the country. They have been replaced by many new groups and families that were small then but have grown exponentially under the changed, freer economic environment.

Even the BSE Sensex, which features the top thirty large-cap companies as a proxy for the universe of listed shares, has been undergoing regular churn. Many companies that weren't anywhere on the horizon a quarter of a century ago, and some that didn't even exist then, now find pride of place on it.

Though many individual companies and business families failed to adapt and fell by the wayside, Indian industry as a whole has prospered. But back then, the future did look grim. Critics alleged that the government had caved in to pressure brought to bear upon it by the United States and by organizations such as the International Monetary Fund and the World Bank. Others called the liberalization process a plot to hand over the country to monopolists, prompting a leading industrialist to quip: 'Even the so-called corporate giants of India are actually pygmies by international standards.'

Freed from the fetters that had bound them for decades, many of my peers began expanding rapidly, often into sectors they had little or no experience in. Not surprisingly, many of these unrelated diversifications failed, forcing them to exit after a few years.

At HSIL, which was still part of the combined Somany Group,

I resisted the temptation to get into new sectors. I had spent my entire life in the sanitaryware industry and was sure that I wanted to stick to the knitting. I was under no illusion that foreign competition would soon be nipping at my heels, challenging HSIL's leadership and hence was more keen to consolidate and expand within the sector rather than fritter away my resources on risky ventures in industries I knew little about.

The company then had an annual turnover of ₹53.77 crore crore, a net profit of ₹1.23 crore crore and commanded a 40 per cent market share. Our main competitors were Parry, part of the south India-based Murugappa Group, and Cera, promoted by Onkar Bhaiji's sons and my nephews Shashi and Vikram.

Sure enough, the big boys of the global sanitaryware industry soon entered the Indian market. American Standard, with which we had come close to signing a collaboration agreement more than three decades before, was the first to do so, followed by Kohler, Roca, Duravit and Toto. Twyfords, which changed its name to Twyford, had by this time ceased to exist as an independent company.

Kohler was by far the most aggressive of the clutch of foreign companies that entered the Indian market and quickly gained market share. Roca bought over Parry in two tranches from the Murugappa Group and this helped it to quickly establish a footprint here.

I commissioned a gap analysis to scientifically assess HSIL's competitiveness vis-à-vis the new entrants. They had brought in a range of high-end items, including the then novel, single-piece water closets.

It took us about eighteen months to grapple with the altered market dynamics. We revamped our design team and launched several new items to meet the competition head-on. Initially, HSIL would import the new items, but we began producing them in-house as volumes picked up.

We also spent a lot of money on beefing up our in-house research and development capabilities, which enabled us to improve the quality of the raw materials we used as well as the glaze on our products—an important determinant of quality. Today, HSIL's research and development department is the only one in the sanitaryware industry that is recognized by the department of science and technology.

Market surveys showed that though HSIL products were at par with those sold by overseas companies in both quality and functionality, the latter were perceived by consumers to be superior. It was a mindset problem—Indians felt that foreign goods were by definition better than those manufactured within the country.

There is only one way to overcome such perceptions—a sustained and well-directed marketing campaign. We strengthened our marketing department, increased our advertising spend and completely revamped our channel relationships. We also launched shop-in-shops, spent money on renovating showrooms and launched our own display outlets to improve customer experience and establish direct contact with the end consumer.

I had, by this time, handed over the day-to-day charge of several operational aspects of managing HSIL to Sandip. I was very happy that he rose to the occasion and personally led many of the initiatives that transformed HSIL into a lean and mean fighting machine that has held its own in the face of intense domestic and global competition. Indeed, facing the market turmoil so early in his career helped Sandip become a better manager.

We also changed our brand name from H Vitreous to Hindware and launched a major print advertising campaign showcasing our products to reach out directly to customers and create a brand pull. In 1995, we began advertising on television.

We held a share of about 40 per cent of the organized market in 1991 when the Indian market was first opened up to foreign brands. Our efforts and the dedication of the entire team at HSIL has allowed us to retain a similar market share even twenty-five years later.

In 2000, I entered into my second foreign collaboration, to distribute Grohe of Germany, Europe's largest bathroom fittings brand. The collaboration lasted five years, at the end of which Grohe entered the Indian market on its own. Our efforts at helping the brand establish its presence in India had only led to the entry of another competitor. Our market share, however, hasn't changed much. So presumably, Grohe's entry must have resulted in lower shares for some of our competitors.

The perceived superiority of foreign brands, however, remains embedded in the psyche of Indian consumers. In 2012, HSIL launched a premium brand called Queo. Though it is owned by HSIL, Queo is registered in England, making it a legitimate foreign brand. Hopefully, this will enable us to change the mindset of Indian consumers with regard to the spurious superiority of all things foreign.

The sanitaryware industry in India still depends greatly on manual processes to ensure quality. There were concerns in the initial years after 1991 that foreign companies, with far higher levels of mechanization, would roll all domestic competition over. Fortunately, worker productivity is high. And mechanization does not pay back before at least five years, rising to six to seven years in some cases. This is why HSIL has not gone in for complete mechanization of the production process. Despite this, I have begun the process of increasing the level of mechanization as trained workers are difficult to find, especially during the harvest season when worker absenteeism can rise to 55 per cent.

HSIL is the market leader in India and has held on to this position for almost half a century. As I've mentioned previously, I have been pleasantly surprised to find my products in use in Pakistan and Africa, and unpleasantly so, to see my brand registered by an unauthorized party in China. At one time, HSIL commanded a 90 per cent share of the Kenyan market. But I have never focused on the export market because both my plants are located in the hinterland—in Haryana and Telangana. The cost of ferrying my products to the west or east coast is prohibitively high. So, exporting to foreign markets is not financially viable for the company.

The government has launched an ambitious project called the Delhi-Mumbai Industrial Corridor to connect the two cities via a high-speed freight corridor, which will run not far from my factory at Bahadurgarh in Haryana. This is expected to lower the cost of freight movement. Whether this will make it feasible for HSIL to export goods is something that Sandip will have to take a call on.

Not only did economic liberalization increase competition in the Indian market, it also brought in foreign investors, who now hold significant stakes in many Indian companies. They demanded greater levels of transparency and much higher standards of corporate governance than were prevalent in India prior to 1991. Simultaneously, the government has also been striving to raise compliance levels in the Indian corporate sector to standards prevailing in more developed economies.

Thus, over the past couple of decades, Indian companies have had to re-engineer many processes and procedures to bring them in line with new laws that mandate improved governance standards and meet the demand from stakeholders to share far greater amounts of relevant information than Indian managements have been used to sharing.

As a result, many companies have had to go through difficult changes. As I've written earlier, I have always insisted on filing returns well within the due dates and on scrupulously following every law in the book.

Additionally, the company has always had a professional and independent board. It has never had more than two family members as directors. Initially, Bhaiji and Onkar Bhaiji represented the family on the board. Subsequently, following the division of the family's assets among four brothers, Sandip and I took their places. Every other director on the HSIL board is independent and non-executive.

We discuss every issue threadbare and Sandip and I continue to report to the board. HSIL's annual report had always given stakeholders much more information than was mandated by law. We continue this practice even today. The goal was, and remains, to stay ahead of the curve.

Many of my peers would often ask why I shared so much 'unnecessary information', especially as most shareholders didn't even bother to look beyond the profit and dividend figures. But I have resolutely stuck to my belief that I have a fiduciary responsibility to all of HSIL's stakeholders to provide all material information about the functioning of the company.

But even though HSIL was already among the top companies in India on corporate governance standards, we had to improve our functioning even further. We brought in more qualified people and strengthened our legal and secretarial departments to ensure total compliance.

I am well aware that competition will only increase and that we will have to be more nimble-footed to tackle any future threat to our leadership position in the Indian market. The going will get more difficult if, at some point in future, the company decides to venture into the export market.

It is not always possible to factor in all challenges that might arise in the future. So my effort has always been to put in place systems and processes that equip HSIL to meet any of the unknowns that are bound to surface from time to time.

12

MY WORK ETHIC AND BUSINESS PHILOSOPHY

I am now seventy-eight years old but still maintain a very intensive work schedule that often stretches to eighteen hours a day. This is because I like to delve deep into every issue and listen to and understand everyone's point of view before arriving at a decision. And as I have said earlier, I like to roll up my sleeves and get my hands dirty.

Some people might say I'm a 'control freak', but I don't care. This is a method that has served me well; I see no reason to change my style of functioning or to do things differently. The Americans have an apt, if inelegant, saying: 'If it ain't broke, don't fix it'. I like to delegate responsibilities, but set milestones that I track to ensure that individuals are working in unison towards the overall corporate goal that is set by the board of directors.

BRINGING THE RAINBOW

I always bear in mind Twyfords chairman Jack Hay's prophetic words that the sanitaryware industry will yield profits only if there is proper supervision. A well-run company is like a well-kept garden. It needs constant and regular nurturing. Take your eyes off it and things can begin to fall apart very fast.

In keeping with this philosophy, I put my son Sandip to work on the factory floor for six months when he joined the business twenty-seven years ago, and then gradually brought him into marketing, product development, and other functions. When I suffered a heart attack in July 1991 and underwent an open heart surgery in May the following year, he was ready to take on the greater responsibilities that were thrust upon him.

Since then, I have ceded more ground to him and other members of the senior management. Now, I retain only policy and strategic direction under my direct watch, though I do still keep an eye on other critical departments. As a result, only three people report directly to me—the HSIL company secretary, the internal auditor and my secretary.

In the tradition of all the great Marwari businessmen I admire, I believe that cash is king. Every transaction, every move, every decision we take has to be cash positive. HSIL now has eight factories across the country and one in the United Kingdom. These are placed under four broad divisions—the building products division, which houses our sanitaryware and other bathroom fittings units; the packaging products division, which has glass containers, PET bottles and security closures under it; the consumer products division, which markets geysers, water heaters, air purifiers and wellness products like shower cabins; and the pipes division.

Each factory is in the charge of a president, who, for all practical purposes, runs the unit under his charge as a chief executive officer.

Every night, each president sends me a report about his factory, detailing the sales, receivables, expenditures, dispatches and dues. I make it a point to go through each report every morning, but usually don't comment unless I find some anomalies or other issues. These interventions are rare and more the exception than the norm. Most of the presidents at HSIL have been with the company for a long time and have played an important role in making it what it is. I, therefore, don't like interfering with their day-to-day functioning since every individual has his own style of working. Stepping in when it is not warranted by the situation would only lead to loss of efficiency and a lowering of morale.

But regular, detailed reporting is an important part of the management information system at HSIL and helps the top management keep close track of every activity within the company and the trends in the market. This also enables us to initiate corrective actions early if the situation calls for it.

I have seen many companies and many institutions go downhill following the passing of the first-generation promoter. These companies were set up and run by their owners as fiefdoms, with all powers centralized under one person. The company succeeded because of the strong personality and management acumen of that individual. The problem with such personality-driven companies is that its systems—the nuts and bolts that define a company's inner workings—are usually weak. When that driving force is removed from the helm, the second rung of management finds itself ill-prepared to take the legacy of success forward. Soon, competitors and rivals get the better of it in the highly competitive and cut-throat world of business.

Naturally, I do not want HSIL to meet the same fate. My board is completely independent. Sandip and I are the only executives on the board of directors. My daughter-in-law Sumita and Giridhari Lal Sultania are non-independent but non-executive directors.

Both Sandip and I report to the board, which deliberates on every issue in great detail. As chairman, I ensure that every member gets his say. Any doubt expressed by any member is clarified in detail. With a 50 per cent stake in HSIL, it would be easy for me to fill the board with friends and associates who would rubber-stamp all my decisions. I know some peers who do that, but I have consciously avoided going down that steep and slippery slope. In this, I am not guided by altruism or goodwill. Jack Welch, the legendary former chairman and chief executive officer of GE (General Electric), who made his company the most admired in the world and retained that position for many years, once said that the secret of his success lay in his strategy of surrounding himself with people much smarter than himself.

I am humble enough to know that I do not have all the answers. The HSIL board comprises men of rare distinction and achievement. It would be foolish not to leverage and take advantage of their combined wisdom and acumen. This is simple common sense, but ego often comes in the way of top management from admitting it.

Another issue I'm punctilious about is compliance. We have to file dozens of compliance reports and remit several statutory dues every month. Nowadays, it has become easier to do so thanks to the computerization of government offices, which allows for online filings.

I have made it mandatory for HSIL executives to file all compliance reports and remit all taxes within the first couple of days of the relevant window being opened. I cannot understand why people wait till the last day to do so. Often, the pressure of handling thousands of last-minute filings leads to servers slowing down or crashing. This can result in missing the deadline altogether, which, in turn, results in the imposition of heavy fines and penalties.

I have instituted a system of green, yellow and red strips to indicate compliance reports and taxes filed and remitted within the first couple of days, on the last day and after the deadline, respectively. Executives who get yellow strips are asked for an explanation. This is intended as a warning to ensure that they don't repeat the 'mistake' of waiting till the last day. The red strip leads to summary dismissal. Readers may consider this unnecessarily harsh, but I don't like the so-called '*chalta hai*' attitude of some executives, since such behaviour easily percolates through the company, lowering efficiency all around. I'm happy to say that HSIL has never missed a single deadline and has been an exemplary corporate citizen through the fifty-five years of its existence.

An important part of management is to ensure that the right man (or woman) is in the right job. The most common method of filling up vacancies when they arise is to promote the executive next in line if his/her performance has been good. This, to my mind, is a flawed system since such promotions are based on performance in a subsidiary role. Good or even exceptional performance in one role does not necessarily mean the executive is ready to step into the shoes of his boss. Just as a great player does not always make a great captain—Sachin Tendulkar comes most easily to mind—a good subordinate does not always have what it takes to lead others. But to deny him or her upward mobility and growth opportunities is also unfair. So, when promoting someone to the position vacated by his boss, I insist that we interview the candidate to test his suitability for the greater responsibilities.

At HSIL, we are very strict about ensuring that all recruitments are based on merit. I sometimes receive requests from friends and acquaintances to recruit a person known to them. I politely tell them that I do not look after or interfere in recruitments and that this is handled by the concerned departmental head and the human resources team.

We consider these requests strictly on merit and do not give any weightage to the name of the proposer. It is not always easy to turn down such 'requests' from influential people, but fortunately, we have managed to stick to our principles without facing any backlash.

I also make it a point never to recruit a friend or relative to HSIL. I am aware of examples where relatives employed in companies have flaunted their connections with the owner to intimidate their supervisors. Progress reports on such relative-employees are often also coloured by the fear of displeasing the owner. In one such case, the actions of the relative-employee caused great embarrassment and losses to the company before he was eased out. I want to avoid such a situation at HSIL. Prevention is better than cure, is an old English proverb that has stood the test of time. I have no wish to fall foul of it.

I do have relatives who are in a weak financial position. I would rather help them with money or in other ways, but will not under any circumstances employ them at HSIL. This reinforces the message that HSIL is a meritocracy and that the promoters do not believe in nepotism.

Similarly, I also strongly believe that it is the responsibility of the top management to ensure a pleasant, cordial and strife-free atmosphere at work. Recently, my secretary told me that a relatively junior female colleague wished to meet me. Her supervisor, it seemed, was harassing her, berating her for real and imagined shortcomings and humiliating her in the presence of other staff members.

I usually don't meet junior staff members—not out of any snobbishness, but because this erodes the authority of their supervisors. It is human nature to approach the highest authority available and allowing executives to bypass the normal chain of command can lead to chaos.

But this was a serious allegation. I had to first ascertain if the harassment had sexual overtones, in which case I would have to terminate the supervisor's employment immediately. But at the same time, I didn't want to meet the complainant in person as it would send the wrong message throughout the company.

So I instructed my secretary to tell the complainant to email her complaint, which I would then peruse. I have an informal system in place that allows me to keep track of what is going on within the company. This channel reported back that while the complaint of unprovoked harassment and humiliation was indeed very real, there was no evidence to suggest any sexual overtones. The written complaint submitted by the complainant also did not contain suggestion of sexual impropriety.

I therefore called the supervisor's boss and told him to sort the issue out, impressing upon him that I had taken great trouble to build an organization that valued its human capital and that any attempt to discriminate or humiliate anyone because of personal biases would not be tolerated. The strategy worked. The complainant emailed my secretary a few days later to say that the problem had been resolved and that her supervisor was no longer picking on her for no reason.

I follow a similar strategy when dealing with labour negotiations or other human resources issues. I never get involved directly in the parleys, leaving the talks to the factory presidents or the authorized executives. I stay in the background, guiding the management and drawing the red lines. Here, too, the reasoning is the same: the authority of the line managers will be seriously compromised if their reportees know they can directly approach the top management. Keeping a buffer between myself and actual events allows me to maintain corporate decorum and discipline throughout the company. Likewise, I make it a point never to call a second-in-command to give instructions as this undermines the authority of his reporting supervisor.

I know this goes against the grain of modern management thinking, which stresses flat organizations where hierarchies are not cast in stone. I feel such a flat organization architecture is more suited for knowledge organizations—such as Facebook or Google and the many start-ups that are mushrooming across India—that depend primarily on human capital to deliver results.

HSIL is a legacy brick-and-mortar company that operates in a very traditional industry. To try and extrapolate the systems of a sunrise industry to one that has a tradition of operating in a particular way would expose it to wrenching change and a transition that it may not be ready for.

A cursory look at the world's leading legacy companies will show that all of them continue to maintain the hierarchies that made them great, though they have simultaneously adopted modern management techniques to keep pace with the times. We do the same at HSIL and as the example cited above shows, have appropriate systems in place to ensure a healthy workplace environment.

I also want to emphasize the importance of discipline, detail and consensus in achieving success in business.

Over the years, I have developed a routine that I follow in order to do justice to the myriad responsibilities that I have undertaken. I usually reach office by 10.30 a.m. every day and spend the next hour-and-a-half going through various reports and other papers. I go through every line of every paper to properly understand the contents.

Many top managers consider this to be laborious and tedious and dub this drudge work, but I cannot overemphasize the importance of this daily chore as it keeps me up to date with developments across my company as well as my industry.

I do not take any calls during this time and avoid meeting anyone unless it is absolutely necessary. Let me give a couple of examples to prove my point.

HSIL recently unveiled a new human resources policy. The document was thirty-one pages long and had hundreds of points. I spent several days with my human resources chief, going through and finalizing each clause. Then, I sent the policy to each of HSIL's five presidents for their comments. They would be the ones implementing the policy, so it was important to get their buy-in. They would be the ones facing any resistance that would undoubtedly arise to some of the clauses and so, would be in the best position to suggest amendments to make the policy acceptable to the greatest number of stakeholders.

I gave them a week to respond with their comments or amendments. That was a long enough time frame for them to go through the new policy in detail and discuss it with their teams. Most importantly, they would not, in future, be able to say that the new policy could not be implemented on the ground and that it had been imposed from the top without consultations.

Such a buy-in is very important. It isn't enough for top management to make policies. Those responsible for implementing them must feel that they have contributed to them and so, have a stake in their successful implementation.

I have come across umpteen examples of companies taking groups of senior managers for offsites to exotic locales to discuss company strategy. The top-level managers will often unveil their vision for the future at such events and tell those assembled that they will have to implement that vision, which is the result of a 'consensus'. What they actually mean is that the vision has been agreed upon by the top management without any effort at soliciting feedback from those who would have to implement that vision.

Very often, the middle managers assembled at these gatherings are not in a position to tell the top management that their vision is impractical or unimplementable. That is why so many vision documents do not lead to the desired outcomes.

I also make it a point to spend time every week reading trade and other journals about the latest developments in my industry not only in India but across the world. This, I think, is one of the most important things I do as it keeps me informed about the latest trends in the sanitaryware industry as well as allied sectors that HSIL has recently entered.

Apart from my job as chairman and managing director, I am also involved in several pro-bono initiatives with various charitable and industrial bodies. As I have mentioned, I have, over my career, been involved in various capacities in The Jaycees, Rotary Club, FICCI, ASSOCHAM, PHDCCI and Indian Plumbing Skills Council, among others.

Regardless of the capacity in which I serve in these organizations, I feel it is incumbent upon me to be thoroughly prepared for all meetings. Consequently, just as I do at HSIL, I read every line of every document that is relevant to the agenda. This enables me to make meaningful contributions and justifiable interventions when necessary.

I have also turned down several offers for positions in organizations and bodies when I felt I did not have the time or lacked the wherewithal to do justice to the job at hand. I have been very clear in my mind that I will not accept ornamental positions or take up an assignment where I am not in a position to make a difference.

I shall end this chapter with an important insight I have gained after a lifetime in industry and in public bodies: top management does not have any time out. It's a full-time assignment where only the most committed succeed.

13

MY IDOLS

When I was growing up and even while I was establishing myself in business, businessmen weren't considered the heroes they are today. Wealth creation was seen as something less than honourable, profit was a dirty word and wealth creators were dubbed monopolists. The logic was perverse, especially in a country with chronic unemployment and debilitating shortages. But that was the prevailing ideology of the times. It did incalculable damage to the Indian economy and perpetuated poverty while benefitting only a small section of society.

Despite the prevailing anti-business milieu, two individuals stood out for their achievements, their probity, their contributions to the Indian economy and to every aspect of public and social life, and their public and private conduct, which allowed them to earn the respect and admiration of millions of their countrymen.

These two gentlemen—J.R.D. Tata, chairman of the Tata Group, and G.D. Birla, the patriarch of the undivided Birla Group—have been my idols from an early age. I have closely followed their careers and tried, in my own humble way, to emulate many of their habits and management techniques. They remain the two business leaders I admire most.

Two other Indian business leaders I admire tremendously are Ratan N. Tata, chairman emeritus of the Tata Group, and N.R. Narayana Murthy, chairman emeritus of Infosys. They are my contemporaries, and though both of them have retired from active business, I continue to hold them in very high esteem. Today, many businessmen are considered national icons, feted by Indian and foreign academic institutions, the media, the political establishment and society at large. This dramatic transformation in the public perception about businessmen was facilitated in no small measure by the achievements and conduct of these two individuals. They gave Indian businesses a global profile and proved to the world that Indian entrepreneurs were second to none.

Two other business leaders I consider my idols are both Americans—former GE chairman Jack Welch and Berkshire Hathaway chairman Warren Buffet.

There are many other industrialists I admire. They include Reliance Industries founder Dhirubhai Ambani, Apple co-founder Steve Jobs, Arcelor Mittal chairman L.N. Mittal, as well as many start-up entrepreneurs in India and abroad, some of whom have already created celebrated multi-billion dollar enterprises in the United States while others are well on their way to taking Indian businesses into uncharted waters with their disruptive practices.

I have had the good fortune of meeting some of my idols in person and learning from them. I have read extensively about the others, their habits and their practices, tried to imbibe lessons from their successes and failures and adapted and used some of their management techniques in my businesses. These have made me a better businessman and made my businesses stronger. I owe them all a huge debt of gratitude.

There are others from outside the world of business whom I consider my idols. Among them, the first name that comes to mind is Mahatma Gandhi. The list of such icons is long and includes Nelson Mandela, Swami Vivekananda, Pandit Jawaharlal Nehru (despite my reservations about his economic policy), Sardar Vallabhbhai Patel and several others. But this book is primarily about my life in business and the people who helped shape it. So, I shall have to regretfully leave out the many non-business icons I so greatly admire and look up to.

J.R.D. TATA

To say that Mr Tata was a successful businessman would be to state the obvious, but my admiration for this pioneer of Indian industry goes well beyond the world of business. Mind you, his achievements in his chosen career are mind-bogglingly great. What else can you say about a man, who, during his fifty years at the helm of the Tata Group, founded Tata Motors, Air India, Titan Industries, Tata Tea (now Tata Global Beverages) and Voltas, even as he took Tata Steel, Tata Power, Tata Chemicals and Indian Hotels Company (which runs the Taj group of hotels) to new heights?

As if the list above isn't enough, he also laid the foundation of India's much-admired software industry when, in 1968, he set up Tata Consultancy Services (TCS) as a division of Tata Sons, the holding company of the group. TCS is now India's largest software services company. Mr Tata's achievements as a pioneer aviator are also too well known to bear repetition here.

To me, even greater than all of the above accomplishments is that he managed to achieve it all without compromising on honesty. It is well known that the Tata Group doesn't bribe politicians and has never indulged in black-marketeering, even though a host of Tata products—from steel to fertilizers to commercial vehicles—did lend themselves to it in the era before economic liberalization swept away shortages. Who knows how much further the group would have grown had it followed these practices that are so common in India.

This is something I have learnt from him and tried to follow in my professional life. As I have mentioned previously, HSIL has de-rostered dealers for overcharging consumers even though well-wishers have counselled otherwise.

In my opinion, Mr Tata's contribution to public life still hasn't been properly appreciated. Despite his preoccupation with the affairs of his large and diversified business empire, he still found the time to set up Tata Memorial Hospital, Asia's first cancer research hospital, Tata Institute of Social Sciences (TISS), the Tata Institute of Fundamental Research (TIFR) and the National Centre for the Performing Arts (NCPA). All these institutes have enriched Indian lives through the decades and contributed immensely to India's public space.

And finally, much before corporate governance became a buzzword in management circles, Mr Tata launched path-breaking initiatives that would be mandated by law only years, sometimes decades, later. For example, it was under his stewardship that his group of companies introduced maternity benefits, gratuity and profit-sharing bonus.

In 1979, Tata Steel, of which he was chairman, launched a new practice under which a worker would be considered to be at work from the moment he/she left home for work till the time he/she returned home from office. Thus, Tata Steel took upon itself the liability for the employee's safety during his/her commute to and from work. Three-and-a-half decades later, this highly progressive and humane labour practice is slowly being adopted by some companies in the West. I don't know of any other Indian company that does so.

But he was simply following a Tata tradition—of being a trendsetter decades ahead of the rest.

G.D. BIRLA

The Marwari community has given India many of its top industrialists. If you take a straw poll in any group of respondents, I have little doubt that Ghanshyam Das Birla, the founder of the Birla industrial empire, will easily emerge as the greatest of them all.

Like Mr Tata, his great contemporary, Mr Birla's achievements go far beyond the world of business. His contributions to the world of primary, secondary and higher education, his massive contributions to charity, his critical funding support to India's freedom struggle and his relentless struggle to take forward the cause of Indian-owned businesses—and not just his own industries—in the face of a hostile administration during the British Raj have all contributed to his legendary status in India's business pantheon.

When Mr Birla, whose first wife Durga Devi was my father's first cousin, entered the world of business, the jute industry in Bengal was dominated by British companies. Indians were treated, as elsewhere, as second-class citizens and tolerated as buying agents and brokers.

Mr Birla's attempts to set up the first Indian-owned jute mill were opposed tooth and nail by the expatriate elite. Undeterred by the opposition from the titans of the jute industry as well as the British Indian government, he succeeded in setting up a jute mill under Birla Jute & Industries Ltd in 1919. He was then only twenty-five years old.

Mr Birla's success prompted many of his peers to follow in his footsteps. Soon, several Indian-owned enterprises were established in the jute industry, but Mr Birla had, by this time, cemented his position as the leader of the pack.

A series of audacious new ventures followed and he emerged as one of India's leading industrialists by the time he was in his early thirties. This was a stupendous achievement by any yardstick, but more was to follow.

A public-spirited individual, Mr Birla had once told my uncle that the biggest contribution anyone could make to society was to spread education and literacy among the masses and especially among women. He used a part of his wealth to found several charitable trusts that set up dozens of schools and colleges across India. The most prestigious among them is undoubtedly the Birla Institute of Technology in his native Pilani in Rajasthan.

He also took upon himself the responsibility of financing a large part of Mahatma Gandhi's political struggle to emancipate India from colonial rule. There is a true story of freedom fighter and poetess Sarojini Naidu once saying, perhaps only half in jest: 'It costs Mr Birla a fortune to keep Gandhi in a state of poverty.'

It says a lot about the man that despite his open support for the freedom movement and his long history of struggle against the

British business establishment, Mr Birla was held in high esteem by the British Raj.

When England's Queen Mary wanted to meet an Indian industrialist in 1943, it was a choice between the two business titans of the time—J.R.D. Tata and G.D. Birla. Lord Wavell, the then viceroy to India, wrote: 'I think Queen Mary would find G.D. Birla better company than J.R.D. Tata if she wishes to invite one of them to lunch. Tata is a pleasant enough fellow [...] (but) much the same as any other wealthy young man [...] Birla, on the other hand, is a less conventional type. He has plenty to say and whatever one might think of Marwari businessmen and their ways, he is well worth talking to. I think Her Majesty would have [...] quite an interesting lunch with Birla.'

Dedication, diligence, perseverance and hard work are the qualities that made Mr Birla the legend he became in his own lifetime.

N.R. NARAYANA MURTHY

If India is considered the technology outsourcing hub of the world today, a large measure of the credit should go to Nagavara Ramarao Narayana Murthy and Infosys Technologies (now Infosys), the company he co-founded with six associates in 1981 with a ₹10,000 loan from his wife.

In many ways, he is the personification of the start-up culture that is currently sweeping across India's business firmament. Only, he preceded it by more than three decades.

The astonishing success he achieved undoubtedly provided an impetus to the current generation of tech entrepreneurs and made entrepreneurship attractive to middle-class Indians, who have traditionally been risk-averse.

By showing that it is possible for six regular middle-class men to start a venture and become dollar billionaires within two decades, he proved that one didn't have to cut corners to reach the pinnacle of success.

Mr Murthy and his co-founders were the first 'rock-star entrepreneurs' of post-liberalization India. By making many of Infosys's shareholders and employees multi-crorepatis and even dollar millionaires—purely on the strength of their shares in the company—he made IT a career of choice for many young Indians.

Under him and some of his successors, Infosys has been rated the 'best employer' by several business publications. This is no mean achievement, especially in an industry where attrition rates are high and poaching of talent, common.

Fortune listed him among the twelve greatest entrepreneurs of our time, while *Time* called him the father of India's IT sector.

I don't know of a single other industrialist who retired from his own companies at the age of sixty. Not only did Mr Murthy and, indeed, all his co-founders do this, but they also gave up all involvement with the company they founded, leaving it in the hands of professional managers.

I know Mr Murthy retains the title of chairman emeritus of Infosys but this, I understand, is purely ceremonial and he is no longer involved in any way in the affairs of the company.

Many business leaders talk about transparency and professionalism but don't always follow it when choosing their biological heirs as successors. Mr Murthy and his co-founders have actually walked their talk and left their company, even though there was no pressure or compulsion for them to do so.

RATAN N. TATA

When Ratan Naval Tata was named chairman of Tata Sons and, in effect, the sprawling Tata Group, many wondered whether he would be able to hold the then disparate group together. Over the years, his predecessor J.R.D. Tata had handed over control of key companies such as Tata Steel, Tata Chemicals, Tata Tea and Indian Hotels Company (which runs the Taj group of hotels) to professional managers who operated more or less independently.

Tata Sons, the holding company, held small, sometimes minuscule, stakes in the main operating companies and it was said that it was only J.R.D. Tata's personality that held the group together. For example, the Tatas owned only 4 per cent of Tata Steel's equity shares. The Birla stake in Tata Steel, in contrast, was 8 per cent. There were very real fears that the 'satraps' who managed the major group companies would break away and form independent professionally managed empires of their own.

This was the scenario when Mr Tata stepped into the very large shoes of his uncle J.R.D. Tata. Like Emperor Akbar, who had to fight and overcome many internal and external hurdles in the sixteenth century before going on to establish the most magnificent empire India has ever seen, Mr Tata's early years at the helm were spent overcoming the challenge from iconic group veterans like Russi Mody, Ajit Kerkar and Darbari Seth.

But once he had established his writ over every company in the ninety-eight-company group, he set about taking his family's then 130-year-old largely India-focused businesses global with an energy and acumen that was and remains unprecedented in this country.

When he took over as chairman, the Tata Group had a turnover of ₹10,000 crore. Its turnover for the 2014–15 financial year was $108 billion (₹7 lakh crore). About two-thirds of this came from abroad.

He started his expansion outside India with the relatively small takeover by Tata Tea of leading English tea brand Tetley in 2000 for £400 million. This was followed in 2006 with a $12-billion takeover of European steelmaker Corus, which catapulted Tata Steel to the fifth rank among steel companies across the world.

Two years later, Tata Motors bought iconic British car major Jaguar Land Rover (JLR) for $2.3 billion from Ford Motor Company. JLR, which was in the red when Tata Motors acquired it, last year posted sales of almost £22 billion, four-and-a-half times its turnover at the time of acquisition, and a net profit of £2.6 billion.

Mr Tata followed up these triumphs abroad with the launch of the $2,000 Tata Nano, the cheapest car in the world. This car didn't do well in the market, but it showcased the can-do spirit and cutting-edge frugal engineering capacity that Mr Tata had built up in his group.

As an Indian businessman, I also revelled in his success. For the first time, a domestic Indian business house was aggressively taking the fight into the world's most developed markets and winning against the best. It was a proud moment for all Indians and was a fitting reply to naysayers who had said economic liberalization would lead to Indian industry being devoured by foreign companies.

Meanwhile, Mr Tata had also transformed the domestic businesses of Tata Steel and other major group companies, turning them into nimble-footed giants that were leaders in almost every industry they were present in.

At the pinnacle of success, Mr Tata decided to walk away from his empire on reaching the group's retirement age for non-executive directors of seventy-five. It would have been easy for him to amend this requirement as his family trusts own 65 per cent in Tata Sons.

But in keeping with his vision of leaving behind a professional group, he not only retired at the designated age, but also handed over the reins of his family empire to a non-Tata.

JACK WELCH

John Francis 'Jack' Welch is, arguably, the most celebrated professional executive in the world. His achievements are immense and his contributions to the world of management, even greater. When he took over as chairman and chief executive officer of GE in 1981, it was another lumbering American giant, stuck in its traditional ways, with a stifling bureaucracy and a market capitalization of $12 billion. When he left in 2001, the company's valuation had risen an incredible 4,000 per cent.

Along the way, he cut through the bureaucracy, sold many old businesses and acquired an incredible 600 companies. His philosophy of either being number one or number two in every industry in which GE was present, or exiting that sector altogether, was revolutionary when he first expounded it, but is now a common practice in many businesses around the world.

He also instituted the practice of firing the bottom-ranked 10 per cent of managers every year. This has been criticized as heartless and anti-middle class. At the same time, he rewarded the top performers handsomely. This enabled him to create a crack pool of manpower that has proved itself over the years, so much so, that much like Hindustan Unilever in India, GE has earned for itself a reputation of being a school for chief executive officers. It also became, during Mr Welch's tenure, the most admired company in the world.

Would Jack Welch have succeeded to the same degree in India?

That's a hypothetical question as the operating environment in India is very different from that in the United States. To begin with, most large Indian companies, with the exception of ITC, L&T, Infosys, and a few others, are family owned. I can't see any of my peers giving a professional manager the kind of free hand Mr Welch got from his board. Then, many of his hard-nosed but good-for-GE policies would have generated a political backlash in India that would have made it difficult to see them through.

But I am hopeful that the coming rounds of economic reforms, currently stalled because of the logjam in Parliament, will create an environment where bright and ambitious executives, who don't necessarily come from business families, can give free rein to their management acumen and create not one, not two, but dozens of Indian GEs.

WARREN BUFFET

I read a lot of business biographies to try and learn from the lives and habits of successful entrepreneurs, practices that can help me run my business. Warren Edward Buffet ranks among the people I admire most, not only because of his credo of value investing, but also because of his frugal personal habits, which, I feel, closely echo my own.

It takes a lot of self-control and strong conviction to be the world's second richest individual and still continue to live in a relatively modest house, which he had bought for $31,000 in 1958, drive his own car and use an old Nokia flip phone.

His business dealings and his investment philosophy are world famous. I, too, have benefitted from his formula on value investing. As I have written in previous chapters, I don't trade in stocks but do invest my personal funds for the long term in companies that offer value over a multi-year horizon.

I greatly admire Mr Buffet's act of gifting 99 per cent of his immense wealth to charity. According to information available in the public domain, Mr Buffet has said: 'I want to give my kids just enough so that they would feel that they could do anything but not so much that they would feel like doing nothing.'

Capturing value, living a frugal life and giving back to society are philosophies that find an echo in the Marwari ethos, which I hold very dear. I have not had the good fortune of meeting Mr Buffet, but his business thinking closely resonates with my own beliefs.

If only more people, and especially business leaders, follow his life's message, society will be the richer for it.

Before I end, I would like to dedicate this chapter to the many business and thought leaders who have influenced my thinking and contributed to my career, who I couldn't acknowledge here, but to whom I owe no less a vote of thanks and a debt of gratitude than the icons I have paid homage to.

14

THE WAY FORWARD

I have worked at the same pace and have followed a similar routine for more than fifty years. During this time, I have witnessed first hand, the dramatic changes that have completely transformed the country's economic landscape.

When I began my career, the Indian economy was marked by shortages in almost everything, shoddy products and very little competition. This allowed HSIL (then, HTL) to quickly establish itself as the market leader, riding on superior technology and industry-leading products.

The situation has changed so much as to be unrecognizable today. Many domestic rivals now produce world-class products. The world's leading brands in this segment, such as Roca, Toto, Duravit and Kohler occupy the top end of the market. Most of them are essentially marketing set-ups that import sanitaryware from factories abroad, including China. Some, however, have set up factories in India. I am happy to report that HSIL has been more than able to hold its own against the global heavyweights.

I don't mind facing up to fair competition, but what really gets my goat is the unrestricted import of cheap Chinese sanitaryware by several competitors for the lower and middle ends of the market. Many of these products compete only on price. They pay little or no statutory dues and undercut the established players. I consider this unfair competition, but in the absence of government action to protect domestic manufacturers, who create jobs and generate taxes for the economy, we have no choice but to live with it.

Over the years, I have handed over several management responsibilities to Sandip and other senior managers. The pace of my work, however, hasn't slowed. I have simply found new things to do and new ways to keep myself engaged.

I now only look after policy and a part of long-term strategy. This takes up only about four to six hours of my time a day. I spend the rest of my day doing pro-bono work, looking after the charitable initiatives I am involved with and fulfilling my responsibilities at the Indian Plumbing Skills Council (IPSC) under the Skills India initiative of Prime Minister Narendra Modi.

I have completed three years as chairman of the IPSC. I may continue for another two years and then step aside for someone else, but will continue to remain a member as I feel that, having been part of the industry from the time it began taking baby steps in the 1960s, I still have a lot to contribute.

Most of my peers and friends have retired from active management, though two of my older brothers remain actively involved with their companies. Many people ask me: 'When will you retire?' My straight answer to that is: 'When God retires me.'

Health permitting, I want to carry on working for as long as I am able to. The logic is simple: I have been a workaholic all my life. I remain curious by nature and try to learn something new every few days. I enjoy meeting people and getting different points of view on topical issues. I feel restless unless I am doing something constructive. I also like passing on the lessons I have learnt from life to people around me.

I have seen many friends waste away after retirement. Time has hung heavy on their hands. Rose-tinted resolutions such as: 'I will catch up on reading', or 'I will spend my time gardening', or 'I will travel the world and see the sights I couldn't earlier', often don't pan out.

I have considered these options and come to the conclusion that I wouldn't be able to survive such a lifestyle beyond the first few days.

This is not to say that I will retain my position at HSIL indefinitely. Quite the contrary. As things stand now, I may hand over charge of HSIL to Sandip after five or six years and focus on the work of the Krishna Somany Charity Trust and the R.K. Somany Foundation, which are doing commendable work and, in particular, empowering women in a variety of ways. My trust supports underprivileged girls, providing them with life skills to enable them to lead a dignified life.

I am also actively involved with the Chirawa College, which was set up by my great uncle a hundred years ago. My family still provides financial support to the college, which many people assume is run by the government because our family name doesn't feature in the name.

There is an interesting story connected with the college. Mahadev Somany, my grandfather's brother, once asked the legendary

G.D. Birla: 'What can I do for charity?'

'There is no greater charity than the gift of education. And there is no bigger way of augmenting the nation's wealth than teaching children, especially girls,' Mr Birla replied promptly.

I started the Laxmi Devi Somany Girls Wing at the Chirawa College in 2007–8 and set a target of enrolling a hundred girl students in the first year. We missed the target and enrolled seventy-eight. Now, 17 to 20 per cent of the 700-plus students are girls.

In Delhi, the Krishna Somany Charity Trust supported the education of a girl from a financially challenged background who recently secured a job at Cisco. This brought tears of joy to my eyes. The trust supports deserving and bright girls from other states as well. It also supports heart surgeries and cancer treatments for people from underprivileged backgrounds.

I take a personal interest in the affairs of the college, fund it and look after a large part of the administration. I intend to increase my involvement with the affairs of my trusts and the college after I pass on the baton at HSIL.

But before that happens, I intend to lead HSIL into some new areas, as we have reached a saturation point in the sanitaryware industry. We command about 40 per cent market share; more brands are entering the market every few months, so there is limited scope for rapid growth.

The prolonged slump in the real estate sector is a cause for worry, since HSIL's fortunes are inextricably tied to the construction and sale of new homes and offices. Realistically, I don't think we will be able to increase our existing market share by much, leaving little margin for growth. That is why HSIL is expanding rapidly into related sectors. Of the four divisions in the company, the mainstay, the building products division, has limited growth opportunities.

Despite this, we are planning to set up a new plant either in Gujarat or Rajasthan for high-end sanitaryware at a cost of ₹80–100 crore. This will be our eleventh plant.

The packaging products division, which had a humble beginning with the takeover of the sick AGI in 1981, is now poised to become an engine of growth. We make glass containers, PET bottles and security closures for whisky bottles. With many new foreign brands entering the market and new Indian products being launched ever so often, I see good prospects for the growth of this business.

Two plants, one for CPVC pipes and the other for safety closures for whisky bottles, are under construction near Hyderabad.

The consumer products division, which is mainly a trading unit, is the one I am most optimistic about. We have launched water heaters, air purifiers and wellness products like shower cubicles, and are also looking at launching a line of domestic electrical appliances.

We sell our geysers under the Hindware Atlantic brand. Atlantic, our collaborator, is a leading French brand. At present, we import the geysers from France and market them under our brand. The initial reception has been encouraging; we sold 15,000 units in the first month itself. We have no plans at present to set up a plant to manufacture these products as the volumes are still quite small. It is thus easier to import them from our collaborator and sell them in India. If volumes rise in the future, we will consider setting up our own manufacturing unit, but that is very much a pie in the sky right now.

Likewise, the consumer products division also imports wellness products from Spain and Italy and sells them under our own brand. We will soon launch water purifiers under the Moonbow brand.

HSIL provides important design inputs to the collaborators to make the products market-ready for India. This is because products designed for the European market may not be suitable for sale here.

All these projects will take time to mature. Unlike the sanitaryware market, where we have a leading position, HSIL is the newbie in these new sectors. There are established brands with long legacies and traditions. We have to break into these markets. That will require patience and fortitude. I would like to stay on at the helm of HSIL to see these initiatives through.

The time is ripe for expansion. India, which was known as the '*sone ki chidiya*' (golden bird) in medieval times, has begun to take wing after centuries of remaining caged. The opening up of the economy in 1991 and subsequent doses of reforms have brought us to the point where we can actually think of turning India into a middle-income country within a generation.

The opportunities are immense. So are the challenges. The election of Narendra Modi as prime minister in 2014 and his well-articulated vision for the country had raised great hopes that India could, perhaps, make that quantum leap very soon. The stalling of his reforms initiatives has caused widespread dismay, but I remain optimistic that India will find a way of overcoming the obstacles that stand in its path. I believe the next decade will offer ambitious Indians and Indian companies tremendous scope for growth.

As the economy slowly picks up and millions of people rise out of poverty, I foresee an explosion of consumption demand that will lead to a manifold increase in the size of the Indian economy. This will throw up many new winners and provide established companies like HSIL many new growth avenues. I will strive to ensure that the company is well placed to benefit from the exponential growth that is just around the corner.

It isn't money that motivates me to grow further. Money is important, but I have never been overly attached to it. God has been kind to me and showered me with plenty of wealth, but I have never consciously chased money. I have never speculated on the stock market, in commodities or in real estate even when friends and well-wishers have advised me to do so. I remain very frugal in my personal life. The money I have is merely a by-product of my efforts in various endeavours.

Meanwhile, my right shoulder, which I had probably damaged during my training in England more than five decades ago and then neglected throughout my life, is now taking revenge on me. For many years now, I have been unable to properly lift my right arm. This necessitated an operation recently, but recovery has been slow. Regular physiotherapy and the daily intake of over a dozen pills to treat this and a variety of other ailments are now a part of my daily routine. Doctors tell me that I have to live with two Ps—patience and painkillers. The message from my body is clear. It is telling me to slow down. That is one of the primary reasons why I have cut down drastically on outstation engagements and other social commitments. But as I have mentioned earlier, my mind is still active and is refusing to heed the call of my body.

I see an incipient trend slowly seeping through the Indian business environment. Owner-managers are stepping aside at some companies in favour of professional chief executive officers. In this respect, India seems to be going the way of the United States, where the children of successful businessmen don't necessarily follow their fathers into the corner offices of family-owned companies.

These heirs have moved from managing companies to managing their wealth while professionals handle the day-to-day affairs of the operating companies. The Wallenbergs of Sweden, the heirs of Walt Disney, some members of the Rockefeller clan and in India, a branch of the Piramal family come to mind.

I do not know if my successors will go that way or will continue as hands-on managers at HSIL. Sandip has made it clear that he doesn't want to work, like me, till his old age.

If I am to be absolutely honest, I will have to admit that HSIL is 90 per cent a professionally managed company. I am consciously avoiding a sweeping statement declaring it fully professional because my son and I still occupy the top three positions and because, given our large shareholding in the company, my grandson, Shashwat, is the most likely successor to Sandip should he want to get involved in the family business.

The board of directors is already completely independent. Both Sandip and I report to the board. And members often disagree with me on various issues. We have heated arguments and I don't always get my way. That is how it should be and that is how we operate. This approach has worked well for HSIL and I see no reason to have it any other way.

I now want to fully professionalize the company so that sometime in the future, I or Sandip can hand over its management to an outside professional chief executive officer as many other business houses are doing.

Shashwat is currently pursuing his BBA at the University of California, Los Angeles. He will probably work as a professional, most likely abroad, for a couple of years before doing his MBA and then, hopefully, join HSIL as Sandip's understudy.

As of now, the indications are that he will follow us into the family business, but one can never be certain with today's generation. Bhaiji's second grandson Srivats, for example, has turned professional. He doesn't want to join Somany Ceramics, which his grandfather had set up and which his father Shreekant now manages. Instead, he worked till recently in a senior position at

Zomato.com, the restaurant-search-and-food-delivery site.

I don't have any particular view on his decision. That is the way the new generation thinks. Tomorrow's India, which I have spoken of earlier, gives youngsters the courage to tread the road less travelled. A century and more ago, our ancestors had left the relative comfort of a settled existence in Chirawa to seek their fortunes in Calcutta, setting in motion the saga of the Somany family. Now another member of the clan has embarked on a similar adventure. Who knows where this path will lead him. I wish him the very best of luck and all success.

But to return to my own plans for the future, retirement is still a distant speck on the horizon. There is still a lot on my plate and I hope to achieve each and every one of the goals I have set for myself, even if it means continuing with my schedule of eighteen-hour work days.

Along the way, I hope to revive my passion for philately and photography. I had given a part of my stamp collection to a nephew many decades ago and misplaced the rest, so I will have to start again from scratch. That will be a new challenge and one that I am looking forward to.

Over the last decade or so, I have also developed a taste for art and paintings. I now own a few paintings by M.F. Husain, F.N. Souza and a few other Indian masters, as well as some canvases by lesser-known artists. My collection began with a few small paintings. Then Sandip began to take an active interest in art and bought paintings by big-name artists. I will, however, stop short of calling myself a collector. I also cannot claim to be a connoisseur. Ours is still just a small selection of artworks that cannot, in any way, be compared to the great private collections that many of my peers have built up over their lifetimes. If the opportunity arises,

I would like to add to our collection, even as I continue my active involvement in the affairs of HSIL, IPSC and my trusts.

I'm getting on in years and hope that my children will retain the warm feelings they share for each other. I have seen many families being torn as under by litigation and intrigue over inheritance, following the death of the patriarch. Over the years, newspapers and television channels have reported in great detail some of the most celebrated corporate battles sparked off by disputed legacies.

I want to avoid such a scenario when I am gone. So I have drawn up a registered will clearly bequeathing my estate to my legatees. I hope that this will help avert any disputes within my family. But I hope that day is far into the future, as I still have a fairly large bucket list of things I want to do.

And what about a work-life balance? We have a once-in-an-epoch opportunity to build the India of our dreams. Each of us has to play a small part in it. I have already defined what I have to do. When all that is done, future generations can enjoy their work-life balance.

ACKNOWLEDGEMENTS

This book would not have been possible without the help and support of my family members and well-wishers.

I would also like to express my gratitude the entire Hindware family, for their unstained support in all my endeavours.

I want to thank Arnab Mitra, for helping me write the book.

My editor Dibakar Ghosh and my publishers Rupa Publications India, for making this book a reality.

And most of all, am eternally grateful to Hiralall Bhaiji and Kamla Bhabi, for being my foster parents.

A family get-together, 1946. Left to right: C.K. Somany (brother), M.K. Daga (nephew) and R.K. Somany

Training at Twyfords, 1961

L-R: G.L. Mehta (Chairman, Industrial Credit and Investment Corporation of India), H.L. Somany (brother) and N.R. Hancock (Manager, Twyfords) at Hindware's Bahadurgarh plant, 1962

R.K. Somany with Sardar Pratap Singh Kairon
at the inauguration, 1963

The outside of a kiln, 1965

Kiln car carrying sanitaryware (before firing), 1965

Kiln car carrying sanitaryware (after firing), 1965

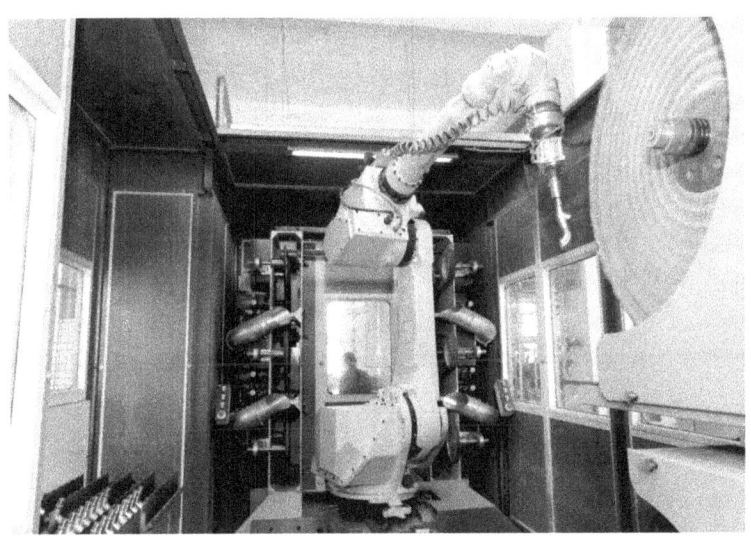

Robotic grinding and polishing unit at the Kaharani plant, 2016

R.K. Somany with son Sandip, 1965

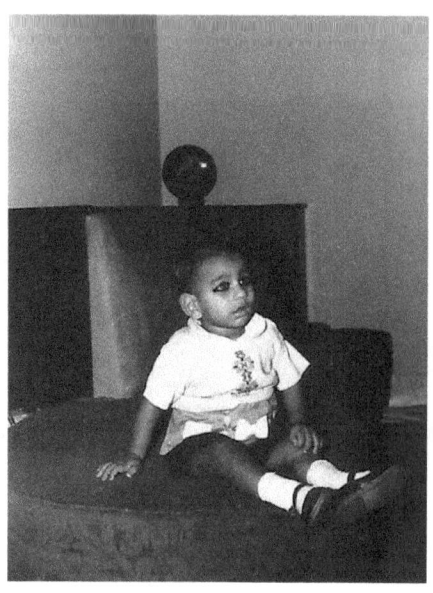

Sandip as an infant

Sandip and Sandhya (daughter)

Sandip and Sandhya at Vijay Chowk, New Delhi, 1972

Sandhya admiring flowers at Vasant Vihar residence, 1973

Sandip (on extreme right) with cousins, 1975

R.K. Somany receiving the National Safety Award from former President of India, N. Sanjiva Reddy, 1976

R.K. Somany receiving the Capexil Certificate of Merit for Exports (1979–80) from the then Minister of Commerce, Pranab Mukherjee

R.K. Somany with Sandhya, Divya (daughter), Snehlata (wife) and Sandip

L-R: Dr R. Venkataraman, former Vice President of India, at the wedding of Sandip and Sumita, January 1987

Visiting the Great Wall of China with wife Snehlata, 1998

L-R: Divya; Sandhya with her son Udish and husband Arvind Agrawal; Snehlata; R.K. Somany

Receiving an award from the then Minister of Commerce, V.P. Singh, 1976

R.K. Somany welcoming former Deputy Prime Minister L.K. Advani at the ceremony where he took over as President of ASSOCHAM, 2002

R.K. Somany leading the ASSOCHAM delegation during former Prime Minister Atal Bihari Vajpayee's visit to Thailand, 2003

At the 92nd International Labour Conference, Geneva, 2004

Welcoming former President of India, Dr A.P.J. Abdul Kalam at the Distinguished Service Awards ceremony of Rotary Club of Delhi Midtown, 2007

Receiving the Superbrand Award, 2007

Hot air ballooning in Turkey, 2008

L-R: Sushila and Sarla, sisters of R.K. Somany, at the centenary celebrations of Chirawa Senior Secondary School, Rajasthan, 2013

Members of the Somany family at the helipad at Chirawa for the centenary celebration of Chirawa Senior Secondary School, 2013

Three generations of the Somanys: R.K. Somany with grandson Shashvat and Sandip at their residence in New Delhi, 2016

The entire Somany clan at 60th wedding anniversary of H.L. Somany, 1985

Printed in the USA
CPSIA information can be obtained
at www.ICGtesting.com
LVHW021947130824
788119LV00005B/57/J